"This wonderful book is a treasure trove filled with gems of meaningful, important information and guidance. For those who struggle with 'the Beast' of depression, Horwitz provides valuable advice that is candid and practical. The 'no-nonsense' language cuts through the haze of jargon and technical talk, offering an accessible road map to remission and recovery."

—**Robert N. Golden, MD**, dean of the School
of Medicine and Public Health, and processor
in the department of psychiatry at the University
of Wisconsin-Madison

"Horwitz knows just how miserable men with severe depression feel. A clinical psychologist, he tells specific things a man can do to feel much better, without telling the lie that depression is easy to fix. He explains what is going on in the brain that keeps depression alive and how behavioral changes can reduce depression. His tone is conversational; his message is direct. I plan to buy a stack of this book and hand it to men I know who need to read it. "

—**Barbara J. Myers, PhD**, associate professor emerita
and former director of the developmental psychology
division at Virginia Commonwealth University,
Richmond, VA

"Horwitz's powerful, no-nonsense guide for men experiencing severe depression is written with sincerity and compassion as he navigates a subject too often ignored. Depression is a serious illness and one of the top risk factors for suicide. Horwitz's passion for this subject can be seen on each page as he provides practical, solution-based options for those struggling with the 'Beast.' It is, without a doubt, a book to share with your colleagues, clients, and loved ones."

—**Julie McIntyre, LCSW, MSW**, retired clinical
social worker for the department of psychiatry
and emergency medicine at The University of
North Carolina at Chapel Hill

"This brilliantly designed book could only have been written by a psychotherapist who has spent thousands of hours talking with men about depression. Horwitz has achieved remarkable things here. He has distilled the relevant research, and presented it in a straightforward, short, but comprehensive form. The ideas are sound and easy to understand while never being oversimplified. This book provides a source of hope without ever underestimating the size of the challenge of overcoming depression. I think anyone who works with men in any capacity will want a stack of these to present at the right moments."

—**David K. Donlon, LCSW**, psychotherapist in
Chapel Hill, NC, for thirty-five years; president of
the American Academy of Psychotherapists

"Depression—we know it's there, but we can't see it. Jonas Horwitz gives us a brilliant way to 'see' and deal with our depression. Revealing how we unwittingly feed a beast that weighs us down, Horwitz provides a way into—and through—the shadows of depression. Look through the windows of this book, as I have, let go of helplessness, and get on with meaningful living."

—**Rev. Steven A. Ingram, DMin, LPCC,**
pastoral counselor

"This book, *How to Stop Feeling So Damn Depressed*, by Jonas A. Horwitz, is just that: a commonsense, direct, honest, easy-to-read guide for men suffering from severe, debilitating, chronic depression. From the opening paragraph Horwitz communicates directly to the men he is writing for in a way that makes it clear he is all about teaching men specific strategies they can use to gain control over their depression, which he calls 'the Beast.' His guide is creative, personal, educational, practical, and guided by research and years of experience as a therapist."

—**Wendy Kliewer, PhD**, professor and former chair
in the department of psychology at Virginia
Commonwealth University

HOW TO STOP FEELING *So Damn* DEPRESSED

The No BS Guide for Men

JONAS A. HORWITZ, PhD

New Harbinger Publications, Inc.

Publisher's Note

This publication is designed to provide accurate and authoritative information in regard to the subject matter covered. It is sold with the understanding that the publisher is not engaged in rendering psychological, financial, legal, or other professional services. If expert assistance or counseling is needed, the services of a competent professional should be sought.

Distributed in Canada by Raincoast Books

Copyright © 2018 by Jonas A. Horwitz
New Harbinger Publications, Inc.
5674 Shattuck Avenue
Oakland, CA 94609
www.newharbinger.com

Cover design by Amy Shoup

Acquired by Jess O'Brien

Edited by James Lainsbury

All Rights Reserved

Library of Congress Cataloging-in-Publication Data

Names: Horwitz, Jonas A., author.
Title: How to stop feeling so damn depressed : the no bs guide for men / Jonas A. Horwitz.
Description: Oakland, CA : New Harbinger Publications, 2018. | Includes bibliographical references.
Identifiers: LCCN 2018031432 (print) | LCCN 2018033125 (ebook) | ISBN 9781684032129 (PDF e-book) | ISBN 9781684032136 (ePub) | ISBN 9781684032112 (paperback)
Subjects: LCSH: Men--Psychology. | Depression in men. | Cognitive therapy. | BISAC: SELF-HELP / Depression. | SOCIAL SCIENCE / Men's Studies. | PSYCHOLOGY / Psychopathology / Depression.
Classification: LCC BF692.5 (ebook) | LCC BF692.5 .H667 2018 (print) | DDC 155.3/32--dc23
LC record available at https://lccn.loc.gov/2018031432

20   19   18

10   9   8   7   6   5   4   3   2   1   First Printing

Contents

Introduction

What you are holding in your hand is an intensely personal guide. I wrote it specifically for men such as yourself, who feel horrible and want to know if there is anything they can do to feel better. While there are approximately 10 million American men who are at this moment severely depressed (NIMH 2017), this guide is not written for them. It is written for you.

If you are looking for a textbook that summarizes treatments for all the different types of depression, then you have the wrong book in your hands. This is not a comprehensive work of that type, nor does it provide a simple ten-step program that will magically take away all of your problems. This is also not a book for men who are simply feeling down because they had a lousy day, or because their team lost last night. It is not for men who are "out of sorts," or who are "just feeling kind of moody lately." It is specifically for men who experience severe depression.

You and I will probably never meet, yet I wrote this book as though you are sitting right in front of me in my office—as though I am talking directly to you. I feel it is very important to speak about severe depression in a clear, straightforward manner, and I will not cover anything that I think is BS. For example, I am not going to pretend that there is one easy trick you have to learn that will make your depression disappear forever. I don't like it when someone lies to me, such as telling me that severe depression is not a serious, painful experience, so I will offer you the same respect.

If this framework makes sense to you, let me also offer three things that I know to be true. First, you have wrestled with severe depression for many years. Second, you are damn sick of it. And third, the only reason you are reading this book is because you want to know what you can do about it. Is there any way you can *stop feeling so damn depressed*?

The answer is yes. In this guide I am going to teach you *specific things you can do* that will help you feel much better, including strategies to change the chemistry in your brain through exercise and deeper social engagement, as well as clear ways to experience greater meaning in your life. I am also going to tell you about the specific types of behavior as well as the specific ways of thinking that make your depression much worse. For example, you will learn how depression tricks you into drinking and eating large amounts of alcohol, sugar, and saturated fats that flood your brain with chemicals that leave you feeling much more depressed. The more you understand how these things affect your depression, the better you will be at overcoming your depression. The information in this book will help you because the more specific knowledge you have about your depression, the more you will be able to take direct actions to beat it. The more you learn, the more you act, and the stronger you will become.

The idea for this book was born while I was in grad school. Or, more precisely, the idea occurred to me while I was lost in the mountains of George Washington National Forest, where a stranger went out of his way to help me. But let's back up a bit. This was in 1997. Classes in Richmond were closed for Labor Day, and I had gotten up at 4 a.m. and driven west to the mountains of Virginia. My dog, Hopper, and I were at the trailhead by 7 a.m. The plan was to hike a clearly marked loop that would bring us back to the parking lot by early afternoon.

Later that morning there was a tremendous crashing sound in the brush, a few yards off the trail. It may have been a bear or a very loud squirrel, but, regardless, Hopper took off running. I eventually caught him but must have missed a turn in the process. By the time the trail intersected a silent dirt road, the sun was beginning to set. I was exhausted, alone, and lost on a remote unpaved road with no houses visible or traffic to be heard.

Hopper and I walked for another hour until I finally heard the sound of a vehicle coming toward us slowly. I stuck out my thumb and was surprised when the pickup came to a stop. My dog was covered in mud, and in the dusk I must have looked fairly sketchy as well, but the driver listened patiently as I explained what had happened. He said that my car was thirty-five miles away, and without hesitation he said he'd be glad to take us there. He explained that I had hiked into West Virginia, where he was from.

On the drive he asked me about what I did. I told him I was in school studying to become a psychologist, and that I did research on men with depression. He was quiet for a few minutes; then he pointed up a hill, where he said his church was. He said he had stopped going there because he was finding it hard to be around people. He paused for a minute and then asked if it was true that there was medication you could take if you were "lost and feeling down."

He revealed that he had been wrestling with awful depression for years, but he was terribly embarrassed and had never spoken about it. He knew that he was in pain, but he had no idea what was causing it or, most important, what he could do about it.

That was more than twenty years ago, and I still vividly remember this stranger who picked up my filthy dog and me and drove us through the mountains back to my car. I wish I had gotten this man's name. I wish there was another way I could have thanked him. Perhaps if I had been able to give him this book, though it would not have been a final cure, it could have served as a compass and pointed him in the right direction. My hope is that this small book will pay it forward and do the same for you: to help guide you out of your intense suffering and point you in the direction of a much more satisfying life.

How to Read This Book

You are reading this book because you are wrestling with severe depression. In addition to feeling miserable, one of the primary symptoms of severe depression is having difficulty concentrating. Because your ability to concentrate is impaired, it will be difficult for you to get through this book. I encourage you to read slowly—*very* slowly. Don't try to read this book all at once. Take lots of breaks. There is nothing wrong with reading this book one page, or even one paragraph, at a time. Pick it up and put it down as often as you need.

I also suggest that you read this book with a pen in hand. Underline ideas that make sense to you, and cross out the stuff that sounds like BS. Talk back to my words. Tell me when I am wrong, or if something doesn't apply to you. Write in the margins and directly on top of my sentences. Don't be shy in striking out the parts that sound like garbage. The deeper you engage with this book, the more you will get out of it.

This book is not perfect, and I welcome your criticism. Why? Because I believe that the more you fight with this book, argue with it, and even yell at it, the more actively it will draw you in. And maybe, just maybe, you'll try a few of the things I suggest and feel a little better. And despite what your severe depression may be telling you, you *can* feel better.

Chapter 1

What Is Severe Depression?

There are many times when being sad is an integral and vital part of life. Actually, I wouldn't just limit this statement to sadness. I think there are also times when a very "healthy" man can and indeed should become extremely depressed. For example, when you lose someone you deeply love, your soul may be torn in half. The mourning that accompanies this profound loss is indescribable. And then there is the mourning over the transient nature of existence, especially as one focuses on the inevitability of death, which does imbue life with a coat of sadness. It seems that if you allow yourself to be sensitive to the world and its profound suffering, sadness may settle on your skin like a fine mist.

Sadness such as this is not a curse or a trap. It is a natural part of life and the counterbalance to joy. However, severe depression—a darkness that goes on and on and grossly impairs basic functioning—is a condition far beyond temporary, "normal" sadness or grief. The horrific suffering of severe depression drains a man's soul and robs him of his ability to create or to act upon the world. It reduces him down to a spiral of limitless rumination. The day is dreaded and the night is feared.

The word "depression" is used for so many different things, many of which have very little to do with what you may be experiencing. For example, when people are sad for a few hours, they often say they are depressed. Or people might throw out the words "I'm depressed" if they are upset because they didn't get what they want, or if they are just feeling cranky because they woke up on the wrong side of the bed.

"Normal" sadness—a *temporary low-mood* state—such as this is not the same thing as severe depression. It is nothing like what you are going through with your screwed-up sleeping, your constant exhaustion, your endless anxiety, your miserable mood, your ceaseless irritation, your hot anger, your inability to concentrate, the pain that courses through your body, or the darkest feelings of helplessness and hopelessness that you are afraid to tell anyone about. It can be very hard to explain the difference to someone who has never experienced severe depression.

Severe depression is an emotional, behavioral, and physical syndrome made up of a constellation of different symptoms, including negative changes to mood, appetite, sleep, and thinking, as well as how you physically feel (APA 2000). These symptoms work together to significantly impair your daily functioning. It is important to note that there is not just one symptom that defines severe depression, and different men may experience different symptoms at different times. While the intensity of these symptoms waxes and wanes, they are present most of the time and last for many months and often many years. The primary symptom of severe depression is generally feeling miserable. I mean really awful throughout much of every day. You probably would describe your mood as "shitty," "the blues," "down in the dumps," or "feeling low." If you wrestle with severe depression, my guess is you describe it as a pervasive feeling of sadness that has been in your life for a long time.

Severe depression seeks to strengthen and maintain itself by insidiously taking over a man's emotions, thinking, and behavior. Like a vicious retrovirus, it may eventually seek to destroy its host. Severe depression is a formidable foe—but it is one that can be faced, weakened, and eventually overcome. How? It must be treated with respect and battled with effective tools and strategies.

Typical Symptoms of Severe Depression

Here are some typical symptoms of severe depression (APA 2000).

You have lost interest in doing things, and almost nothing makes you happy. In addition to feeling miserable most of the time, very few things get you really excited or make you truly happy when you suffer from severe depression. I am not saying you are lifeless and don't do anything at all, but rather that almost nothing—even activities you once enjoyed—gives you any real pleasure, and you have to force yourself to do almost everything.

You have little energy and are often exhausted. When you do motivate yourself to get going, you often have very little energy and find yourself tiring easily. Sometimes it feels as though you are trudging through three feet of molasses. This feeling of exhaustion makes it very hard for you to get anything done and makes it hard to find the motivation to start things in the first place, which leads to greater avoidance of the things you know you need to do, creating more stress and more depression.

Your ability to concentrate is shot. Severe depression makes it difficult to concentrate. *And that difficulty is going to play out as you read this book.* I know that it is hard for you to get through these words, to make it to the end of the page. It is a miracle you have made it this far. If you are having trouble concentrating right now, I want you to stop reading. Put this book down. You have read enough for now. Go do something else for at least thirty minutes. When you are ready, come back and pick up reading at this page. Read this book in small bites. You don't have to go through it all at once. There is also nothing wrong with reading one paragraph again and again. Read a few pages at a time. That is all you have to do.

You feel very irritable a lot of the time and may have angry outbursts. My guess is you are often very irritable and find yourself snapping at people or yelling a lot more than you would like. This irritability often erupts as anger, directed at others or yourself. We often direct anger toward ourselves in the form of endless negative self-criticism. This cycle of self-criticism is a fundamental part of depression, and I am going to focus a lot on this process.

You experience all sorts of physical problems. In addition to generally feeling miserable most of the time, you probably wrestle with a whole series of physical symptoms, such as headaches, dizziness, stomach problems, weight changes, and chronic pain (including muscle and joint aches). Your back may often hurt, you may have the sensation of carrying a heavy weight on your shoulders, and you may feel drained and worn out. Men often do not recognize this connection—how emotions are expressed in the body as physical symptoms—because when we were boys, many of us were socialized to ignore and dismiss our feelings. We were told "Big boys don't cry," "Get over it," or to "Man up!" I am not suggesting that men shouldn't be strong, but admitting that we have a whole host of complex feelings actually takes enormous strength and helps us become much more resilient in the face of great stress. Denying feelings does not make them go away. In fact, the more we deny our sad, depressed emotions, the more likely they are to appear as physical symptoms like stomach problems, headaches, and chronic back pain.

Your appetite is screwed up. Another way severe depression can affect you physically is by changing your appetite. You may either find yourself eating way too much—typically craving unhealthy food that is filled with sugar and saturated fat—and gaining a lot of weight, or you basically have lost your appetite and nothing tastes very good, so that you end up losing a good deal of weight. It is very common for a severely depressed man to want to gorge on junk food, and the more depressed he is, the more junk food he will eat. The problem with junk food is that in addition to making you feel bloated and heavy after eating too much crap, it causes fat to build up around one's stomach and alters the neurochemistry that underlies one's mood, changing it for the worse (Sharma and Fulton 2013).

Your sleep cycle is impaired. When severely depressed you may suffer from insomnia. You may find that you just can't fall asleep, or you may have restless sleep and wake up throughout the night and find it difficult to fall back asleep—especially in the early morning hours. Conversely, many severely depressed men experience the opposite of insomnia, which is called *hypersomnia*—that is, all they want to do is sleep. They end up sleeping ten or more hours a day but still feel exhausted, as if they barely slept. It is not unusual for severely depressed men to go back and forth between periods of insomnia and hypersomnia. In chapter 2, I outline specific strategies you can use to get much more restorative sleep. Sleep is one of the primary foundations of mood, so the better you sleep, the better you will feel.

You have low self-esteem and profound feelings of guilt. Feeling lousy about yourself is another primary symptom of severe depression. You generally view yourself as worthless or "less than" compared to other people. Many of the men I talk with who wrestle with severe depression admit that they hate themselves. They say things like "When it comes down to it, I am just no good. I have nothing to offer. I am an utter failure, a complete asshole." Along with this despair they often express powerful feelings of unremitting guilt. The voice in their mind endlessly repeats things like *I can't believe I did that…* or *I really should have done this…*

If you really listened to yourself speak, my guess is you'd hear the word "should" quite a lot—as in "I really *shouldn't* have done that…" or "I really *should* do this…" The problem with "should" statements is that no matter what you do, you almost always end up viewing yourself as a failure.

The guilt you feel often manifests as a stream of self-criticism. *This stream of self-criticism becomes a constant private narrative, running in your mind like an automatic tape.* You criticize how you look, what you wear, what you said to another person, what you didn't say to another person, what you got done today, what you didn't get done today. This self-critical narrative is a distinctive voice in your ear that goes on and on, like a song on endless repeat. At this very moment, as you read these words, that narrative is most likely whispering in your ear and telling you that there is nothing that you can do, and you don't have the ability to change how depressed you feel. *That voice is wrong.*

You may have thoughts of suicide. Severely depressed men often think about death, not just death in general, but their own. A severely depressed man will often think about killing himself. This is called suicidal ideation, and it is one of the most dangerous symptoms of severe depression. Suicidal ideation presents a strange paradox: because your brain is feeling awful day after day, the only "cure" it may be able to come up with is committing suicide, creating a *permanent* solution for a *temporary* problem.

If you find yourself thinking about killing yourself, get help immediately. Seriously, this book is not enough. Put this book down and call 911 or your local hospital and ask to speak to a psychiatrist. You can also call the 24/7 National Suicide Prevention Lifeline: 1-800-273-TALK (1-800-273-8255). This hotline is staffed by licensed mental health professionals who can help you. You can also find more information at www .suicidepreventionlifeline.org.

Respect Your Enemy

If you only learn one thing from this book, it should be to *take your severe depression seriously*. I know that this sounds odd, even stupid, when you are desperately trying to figure out how to stop being so damn depressed. There is a good chance that what you really want is to be able to just get a break from your anguish and to stop thinking about it, and that is my goal for you as well. Yet the way to become less depressed is to start treating your depression much more seriously. The more seriously you view your own severe depression, the more you can increase your willpower to take action against *the behavioral syndrome* of severe depression, which is the key to defeating it.

A primary way to increase your willpower is to treat severe depression like you would any other serious medical diagnosis. For example, imagine that your doctor tells you that you have severe hypertension (high blood pressure), and, if left untreated, it could lead to a life-threatening stroke. Now imagine walking out of your doctor's office, telling yourself, *Hell, high blood pressure is not really a big deal...* That thought is a way of minimizing your new diagnosis, convincing yourself that you don't have to take it seriously. And because you don't accept that it's serious, you are not going to feel the need to make any changes in your life.

Maybe nothing happens, at least for a while. But as time passes and you continue to minimize the diagnosis, you set yourself up to have a devastating stroke. Imagine what would happen if you walked out of that office and said to yourself, *Okay, it's true, I can't deny it anymore. I've got high blood pressure. And, yes, it's serious, and I am definitely going to start doing specific actions to make it better.* Your outcome would most likely improve greatly.

The same goes for the diagnosis of severe depression: there are specific things you can do that will dramatically decrease your depression. Yet when it comes to feeling down, many men have been trained to minimize and invalidate their symptoms, especially depressed feelings. We are generally socialized to be wary of our feelings, unless they are rage or lust. That is, anger and horniness are considered "real" feelings that men are allowed to experience, while more vulnerable feelings like sadness are often distrusted, pushed aside, and seen as a sign of weakness.

We especially mistrust feeling bad. A voice inside says, *Snap out of it, pull yourself up, stop whining, and get over this crap.* That critical, shaming voice not only invalidates our emotional experience, it also leads us to believe that our depressed feelings are not really serious. And if we don't consider our feelings as serious, then we think there is nothing we really need to do about them.

Severe depression, however, is a very serious condition. This is not something you can just "snap out of," nor is it a condition that you can just ignore and expect to dissipate on its own. It is a condition that has likely made your life absolutely horrible for years on end, and in some cases it may convince you to try and kill yourself. So, yes, I want you to learn to take your own severe depression very seriously and to treat it with the respect it deserves—just as you would cancer, heart disease, or any other life-threatening illness.

The damned thing about severe depression is that it takes over your brain, your spirit, and your soul and makes you feel hopeless. It wants you to say to yourself, *There is nothing I can do to make myself feel better. I am helpless in the face of my problems. I am without hope.* Even at this very moment as you read these words, your severe depression is probably whispering in your ear: *This is all BS. Who the hell is this guy? What the hell does he know about your life? Does he have any idea of the pressure you are under? The problems that you are confronting? The crap you've had to deal with? No, he knows shit.*

Your depression has lived with you for a long time. It has seldom left your side. It is relentlessly pessimistic and wants you to believe that your misery will never end. The more helpless you feel, the less hope you have, the happier your depression is. Your severe depression is your adversary. Treat it with deep respect.

Here is how to begin.

Give Your Severe Depression a Name

In the previous section I encouraged you to take your severe depression much more seriously—that is, to give it the respect that it deserves. However, as you read this book, the voice of your severe depression will be whispering in your ear, *This is all BS!* It has a powerful voice dripping with cynicism and despair. Your depression sits on your shoulder and tries to anticipate your every move. You have lived with that despairing voice for a long time. It does not want you to believe there is anything that you can do that will help you feel better. Yet, at this very moment there is something you can do. You can learn to think about your severe depression in a new way. I want you to conceive of your severe depression as a separate entity. You read that right: picture your depression as something separate from yourself. Turn your depression into an alter ego, or a shadow that lives alongside you. It may help to take a second and close your eyes. In your mind make a picture of your depression. The image of a dark, hulking, fog-like beast works for me, but whatever picture you come up with will also work. This may seem awkward or even ridiculous at first, but please give it a try.

Now give your depression a name. Some of the greatest leaders in history also wrestled with terrible depression, such as Winston Churchill, who called his depression "the black dog" (Attenborough 2014). I've had clients name their own depression "the f*** its!" or "the fear." For the sake of this book, I'll call the image of your depression the Beast, but you can call it whatever you like.

Take this picture of your depression and imagine the Beast squatting in the corner of your life. It goes wherever you go. It is even reading these words right along with you. But the Beast is not you. There is you, and then there is this Beast—two very different things.

The goal of conceiving of your depression as a separate entity is very simple: to help you see that *you are not your depression*. The more a man can picture his depression as something separate from who he really is, the stronger his willpower becomes and the weaker his depression. This change allows him to engage in specific positive actions that will drain energy from his own Beast.

Here's a powerful way to reinforce this process of separating yourself from your depression. Say this sentence out loud: "I am not my depression. There is me, and then there is this damn depression."

I know that this sentiment may make sense to you on an intellectual level, but on a feeling level, deep in your gut, it may seem like crap. That's okay. The idea that you are not your depression—that your severe depression is something separate from who you truly are—takes time to sink in. In the meantime, the Beast is not just sitting there watching. It is also reading these words. And it will do everything it can to convince you that you will always be depressed, that this is who you are and who you will be, and that there is not a damned thing you can do about it.

Your Beast is a liar.

A man is not his depression. To make this crucial concept as clear as I can to my clients, I ask them to physically move over to one corner of the couch in my office. I have a large stuffed gorilla, which looks like a monster, that I seat on the other end of the couch. Then I tell my clients to think of the gorilla creature as the manifestation of their horrible depression.

The Beast does not just live on the couch in my office; it also goes through a man's life alongside him. It goes everywhere he goes. It stays with him throughout the day and the night. The Beast watches TV with him and walks into a convenience store with him. It goes to work with him in the morning, and in the evening it sits beside him as he is stuck in traffic. It is even reading these very words. It is probably whispering loudly, *This is all BS! I can tell already that this is going to be one of those "think positive" self-help books that are full of crap.* That voice sits on your shoulder and tries to anticipate your every move. You have lived with that despair for a long time. It does not want you to read this book. It does not want you to believe that there is anything you can do that will help you feel better. You've probably heard addiction referred to as the "monkey on your back." Severe depression is like carrying a two-ton monkey on your back everywhere you go. But no matter how heavy your depression feels, no matter how long it has been with you, remember: your Beast of depression is not you.

Depression is a powerful physical, emotional, and behavioral syndrome that has insidiously taken over your life, but it is not you. It is not your essence. It is not your core. It is a dense morning fog that has snuck up on you stealthily and taken over your life. The fog may be so thick that it is difficult to see yourself within it—to differentiate yourself from severe depression. But there is a difference between the part of you that is in pain and the part of you that is more than your suffering—the part of you that feels absolutely helpless and the part of you that retains the ability to transform your life and the life of those around you.

I realize there is a good chance that my words may come across like quaint cheerleading. They may be nice to hear, and at best they might apply to someone else, but you believe they are simply not true for you. If that is where you are, then you are right on target—in that you are right. We are strangers. I do not know the specific problems you are dealing with, but I do know that wherever you go, your Beast of severe depression is right beside you. I know that it is reading these words and doing its best to make you feel over-whelmed, helpless, and out of control. I also know that even though your severe depression is a powerful son of a bitch, *it is not invincible.*

Your Beast is vulnerable, and I am going to teach you specific techniques that you can use every day to combat it. These techniques do work. They will drain energy from your Beast and significantly reduce its power over your life. The more you implement these strategies, the better you will feel.

Before moving on to the next section, be sure to do the following:

1. Conceive of your depression as a separate entity.

2. Draw a picture of your severe depression in your mind.

3. Name your severe depression

And for good measure:

4. Remember this thought: *wherever I go, the Beast will try to go with me.*

5. Never forget: The Beast is your adversary.

6. Now think of this idea: Your Beast, your severe depression, is your enemy. It may appear strong, but it is not invincible. It is vulnerable.

The Nature of the Beast

In order to combat any enemy, you must understand its nature. The better you understand your severe depression, recognizing what it wants and what makes it tick, the better armed you can become to resist its demands and loosen its hold on you. So what is the nature of the Beast? What is the one thing that your Beast always wants?

Your Severe Depression Only Wants to Get Stronger

The most important thing to know about your Beast is that it will do everything it can to get stronger. Your Beast doesn't want to go away, it doesn't want to be cured, and it doesn't want to be something that you used to have to deal with. *Your severe depression wants to get stronger and stronger.* It wants to take over. It wants to convince you that you are helpless, that there is no hope. Think I'm being ridiculous? Then why is it whispering in your ear? *Stop reading this shit. Get a beer. Turn on the TV. Play a video game.* Your Beast will not wander away on its own. It will not get lost. It will not abandon you. The goal of severe depression is to consume your life. Your Beast will do everything it can to take over your thoughts, your emotions, and your behavior.

Severe depression is an all-consuming syndrome that seeks to feed itself. Its aim is to increase its own strength, and this means making you more isolated, more alienated, and more in despair. Your Beast wants you to feel as miserable as possible. It will do everything it can to get you to engage in behaviors that make you feel awful. In fact, in order to survive, your Beast needs you to engage in behaviors that give it energy. This need for energy is precisely where the Beast is vulnerable. The way to stop feeling so damn depressed is to take away its energy—to stop engaging in the behaviors that leave you feeling more miserable. The more you starve it, the better you will feel.

Your Beast is smart, and it knows that the best way to trick you into engaging in behaviors that make it stronger is to slide in when you don't see it coming, when you are most vulnerable and open to suggestion. These vulnerable moments happen when you are dealing with a problem you think you can't cope with—that is, when you are highly stressed.

Your Beast sits on your shoulder waiting for you to run into problems that you feel are out of your control. As you get more stressed and more tense, it whispers, *You need a break, an escape, to blow off some steam.* These thoughts typically come across as reasonable. Everyone needs to take it easy now and then. If you keep going full throttle, you may end up having a heart attack. But here is the sly trick: the very behaviors that the Beast wants you to engage in, which appear to be a simple and easy way to take a break from your depression and blow off some steam, like drinking, smoking pot, eating junk food, or mindlessly watching electronic screens, actually have the opposite effect. They create the exact thing you are trying to cure. These self-numbing behaviors may work temporarily but then directly increase how depressed you will feel by creating a rebound effect. This is the process that happens during the following twenty-four to seventy-two hours, when your feelings of depression and despair rebound and come roaring back at you.

Stop here for a second. The Beast is also reading these words and is likely whispering in your ear: *I told you this was all crap... "the Beast," "energy," "taking over your behavior"? What kind of BS is this guy talking about? If he only knew the hell you were going through, he would see that the reason you are down is because you have horrible problems. Does he know about the problems you are having at work? Or what is going on at home? Does he know about the crisis in your relationship? Does he know just how horribly lonely you are? I bet his health is great and he doesn't have to worry about paying the bills. What the hell does he know? He knows nothing about your past. He knows nothing about the crap that you have been through. He knows nothing about what you are trying to deal with right at this moment.*

Remember how I said I was going to be straight with you and not give you any BS? Well, this is what I know from years of experience treating men with severe depression. I know that your Beast is telling you that the reason you are so depressed is because of all the terrible problems in your life: your money problems, your job problems, your relationship problems, your health problems…etc. But it is not these problems that have made you severely *depressed*. What they have made you is severely *stressed*. What has made you horribly depressed are the ways in which you have tried to deal with these problems. This is a crucial difference that bears repeating: The problems you are facing have made you severely *stressed*, not severely depressed. What has made you severely *depressed* is the way your Beast has encouraged you to cope with them. The ways you have tried to cope with your problems are not effective. They do not solve your problems. Instead, they create more problems for you, and you end up feeling even more miserable.

So what he is saying is that you not only have a shitty life, but are a failure in how you cope with it… If this is what the Beast is telling you, then you can be sure you are on the right track, because it desperately does not want you to figure out that there are ways to cope with your problems that will significantly reduce your stress. Your Beast also doesn't want you to figure out the ways it is getting you to avoid your problems, because avoidance leaves you feeling even more depressed. The Beast is activated when you are stressed out by a problem, and then it tries its best to get you to do things to make the problem worse.

Problem

Take a moment and picture your severe depression, your Beast, as this dark fog-like monster quietly lurking in the corner of your existence, in the shadows of your life. It is sitting there silently watching as you go through your life, and it is waiting. It is waiting for you to run into stress. Not just any stress: it is waiting for you to run into stress you feel you can't cope with. When you encounter problems you feel you can't deal with is the moment when your Beast sits up and smiles. This is exact moment it has been waiting for. This is the moment it can now go to work and start whispering in your ear, *For God's sake, you need a break. Go ahead and blow off some steam. Your life is too hard. You need an escape, even if it is just for a little while.* Yet the specific things it encourages you to do to get relief from your problems are the exact things that are making your severe depression much worse.

In summary:

- The goal of your Beast is always to get stronger.

- The primary method it uses to strengthen itself is to trick you into engaging in behaviors that make it stronger.

- It starts whispering in your ear when it sees you are stressed, experiencing problems you are not sure how to cope with.

- It tells you that you need an escape, and it desperately wants you to believe that this escape will make you feel better.

- These escapist behaviors initially appear like they will help you blow off steam, but they end up creating a rebound effect that leaves you much more depressed.

- The problems you are facing have made you severely stressed, not severely depressed. What has made you severely depressed are the ways you have coped with these problems, which the Beast has encouraged.

- It is the specific "blowing off steam, just need an escape" behaviors that feed your Beast with the energy it needs to get stronger and make you feel worse. The more your Beast is fed, the worse you will feel.

What Feeds the Beast?

One of this guide's goals is to teach you how your severe depression, your Beast, has tricked you into doing things that leave you feeling more and more miserable. Your Beast is hungry. It wants to be fed, and it will do its damnedest to tempt you. It will whisper in your ear that you are exhausted and have no energy, that the only thing you can do is "nothing." By "nothing" it means to avoid taking any positive action; just sit there and keep playing video games, endlessly surfing the Internet, or mindlessly flipping through the TV channels. Your Beast wants you to remain as passive as possible: don't create, don't act upon the world, and don't do.

It can sometimes feel like these impulses are impossible to ignore, but the reality is that your depression's need to be fed is its weakness. Just like you, the Beast requires energy to sustain itself. When you rob your severe depression of its energy sources, you will drain the Beast of blood. Your depression will begin to weaken, and you will feel increasingly better.

Your Beast encourages you to engage in numbing behaviors and avoidance strategies, such as drinking and not facing stressors head-on, and these tactics leave you feeling more depressed. The more depressed you feel, the more energy the Beast has to feed on. The more you feed the Beast, the worse you feel. This repetitive cycle leaves you exhausted and in despair. The way to break this cycle is to stop feeding the Beast. Stop giving it energy. One of the most basic ways your Beast gets more energy is to trick you into flooding your brain with chemicals that directly cause depression. Let's start with the most common chemical: alcohol.

Alcohol and Your Severe Depression

The number one chemical that energizes severe depression is alcohol, or ethanol (Boden and Fergusson 2011). It does not matter the form. Craft beer, light beer, bourbon, vodka, gin, tequila, whiskey, mixed drinks, red wine, white-wine spritzers, hard cider, Jell-O shots—you name it, these all contain alcohol. The concentrations of the ethanol molecule in each may vary, but the net effect is the same: *all* types of alcohol cause depression.

Your Beast loves it when you drink alcohol and wants you to drink as often as possible. *Hold on a second,* you might be thinking, *a cold beer on a hot day does not cause severe depression.* You are both right and wrong. You are right in thinking that one cold beer on a hot day does not *cause* severe depression, but this is true only *if your brain is not traumatized.*

However, if you are experiencing severe depression—if you are so miserable that just about everything feels horrible, nearly everyone gets on your nerves, your body hurts, your sleep is messed up, and you practically have to drag yourself through the day while at the same time wishing you were dead—then your brain has experienced significant trauma. It has been wounded, and it is under a severe amount of stress that it can't figure out how to cope with. The ethanol molecule in all alcohol is a neurotoxin that is poisonous to the brain (Brooks 1997). It is a depressant compound, and it will make your severe depression much worse.

If you don't drink, great. Skip this section. If you do drink and you want to keep drinking, that is your business. The world is flooded in alcohol. It seems to have always been that way and most likely always will be. I'm not here to tell you whether or not you should drink. That is completely up to you. But if you want to stop feeling so damn depressed, that is my business, and I can show you specific strategies that change the chemistry in your brain and will help you start feeling better now.

I am not writing this guide as a way to control you. Like most people, you are going to do what you want to do. However, as your personal guide, I want to show you the intimate relationship between your severe depression and alcohol consumption. The alcohol you are putting into your brain is making you feel worse. Like many chemicals that cause depression, its relationship with the brain is extraordinarily tricky.

In terms of your severe depression, I want you to picture your brain as having a significant gash, a gaping wound. The ethanol molecule acts as a neurotoxin; specifically, it impairs the stability of the architecture in your brain that regulates mood (Ma and Zhu 2014). Pouring alcohol (which is classified as a depressant compound) into your brain is like pouring sulfuric acid into a gaping wound on your thigh. It makes the wound a whole lot worse. That is why the Beast is trying its best to get you to drink, because it knows that the chemical changes in your brain caused by the alcohol will make you feel more depressed—and help it grow stronger.

Alcohol is tricky. After your first drink, you generally don't feel searing pain or a horrible spike in depression. If it were only that simple—as in, take a drink and scream in agony—you probably wouldn't end up drinking so much, would you? The initial drink has the effect of dampening, or depressing, your symptoms of depression. This dampening happens in two ways: First, small amounts of ethanol initially stimulate the production of the neurotransmitter dopamine in your brain (Ma and Zhu 2014), the brain chemical associated with feelings of pleasure. For a limited period of time you will feel a bit better as the dopamine activates your brain's reward centers. Second, as the ethanol floods your brain, you may temporarily experience a reduction in anxiety. Feelings of anxiety are very common in severe depression, and for at least a couple of hours or so alcohol molecules do a pretty good job of suppressing them because they mimic the effects of the neurotransmitter GABA (gamma-aminobutyric acid) (Banerjee 2014). When GABA is activated in the brain it generally makes us feel less anxious. So at least in the beginning, the drinks leave you feeling better.

But then there is the rebound. The lousy feelings of depression and anxiety come roaring back with a vengeance anywhere from twenty-four to seventy-two hours after you drink a substantial amount of alcohol. Your mood will plunge, your problems will seem much worse, and you will be left feeling more hopeless.

Stop here for a second and focus on this word "rebound."

The rebound is not just a hangover from being dehydrated or the result of having one too many. It doesn't happen just because you drank the wrong type of

booze. This rebound is an integral part of the chemical process that results from the neurotoxin ethanol flowing into your brain and central nervous system. And the rebound *always* acts as a shot of adrenaline to the Beast, allowing it to inflame your feelings of irritation, hopelessness, and despair. The ethanol you consumed has lowered the levels of the neurotransmitters serotonin and GABA that your brain uses when it tries to cope with stress (Banerjee 2014). Every problem will appear much, much worse during the rebound. Every stressor will appear insurmountable. Your life will appear hopeless. This is exactly what the Beast has been desperately waiting for.

If you are a man with severe depression who drinks, my strong guess is that you are drinking a lot more than one beer or an occasional glass of wine. If you told me you liked beer, I would guess that you drink anywhere from three or more beers a night when you do drink, and then much more on the weekends. Do you go through a case of beer on the weekends? Maybe sometimes, sure. Why not? But most likely you don't drink every night. Days go by when you don't drink anything. That is why the Beast is right now whispering, *I told you, this guy doesn't know what he is talking about. You don't abuse alcohol. You are not an alcoholic, hell no. You only drink at dinner, or on the weekends, or when you are with your friends.*

Is the Beast reminding you right now that you have a set of rules that regulate your drinking, and that sometimes you even stick to them? *No drinking before 5 p.m. No drinking hard liquor. No drinking alone. Or no getting drunk in public.* Perhaps it is saying something like *You can stop anytime you want. Just last winter you made a decision not to have anything, not one drink, after the Super Bowl right up to St. Patrick's Day. Five weeks, no booze—not even a beer, nothing. That proves it. You don't have a problem with drinking, and you have proven that you can stop anytime you want.* Or are you right now thinking about someone else who is a "real" alcoholic? Perhaps a relative or friend "who really drinks" or the poor guy on the street drinking out of a paper bag? *These are the guys who are addicted. They are the ones with the problems. Not you.* And so the whispering continues.

Well, perhaps the Beast is right. Perhaps you don't abuse alcohol, and it has no real effect on your mood. Perhaps your drinking has nothing to do with your horrible depression. If that statement is true, then you probably would not feel any anxiety if you said to yourself, *You know, I do have severe depression. I am going to take this seriously, and I am going to think of my brain as having a major gash. Because I have this wound in my brain, I am going to stop pouring alcohol—a depressant compound—directly into it.* If you do notice yourself getting anxious the more you think about not drinking, that can help you understand how much you are using alcohol to self-medicate and numb yourself from your stress. Alcohol may be giving you the illusion of coping with your problems, but the chemical is damaging your brain and exacerbating your depression.

Here is an image to think about if you are trying to drink less. Picture the small, dark-yellow pill bottles that your medicines come in, the ones with a white label and a childproof cap. Now in your mind's eye, imagine there is a pill bottle filled with an antidepressant in the medicine cabinet in front of you, but right next to it is another yellow bottle, an empty one. Take the cap off the empty one and pour a drink into it. Anything that has alcohol in it will work. Now imagine that drink has been dehydrated so the liquid has been removed and all that remains are pills made of alcohol. One bottle contains antidepressant medication and the other contains chemicals that cause depression—a "depressant medication." Every time you have a sip of alcohol, think about this image and how the alcohol pills are making your depression much worse.

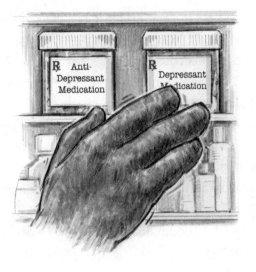

ALCOHOL AND SEXUAL DESIRE

In addition to directly making your depression much worse, alcohol damages your nervous system, leading to a loss of sexual desire and impotence. Over time, those delicious cold beers reduce the amount of testosterone your body produces (Emanuele and Emanuele 1998). This leads to increased feminization in men, such as developing "man boobs," which is a primary symptom of cirrhosis of the liver. Does it sound like I am trying to scare you? I really don't think you scare that easily, but I do think you should know about the adverse effects of the chemical you are self-medicating with.

ALCOHOL AND SLEEP

I have heard many depressed men say, "The real reason I drink is because it helps me go to sleep." I agree that for many men, alcohol does seem to knock them out, and at least temporarily dampens their baseline anxiety, leaving them groggy. Yet this anxiety alone isn't what is causing the insomnia. They can't fall asleep in the first place because alcohol abuse has already impaired their sleep cycle. It has *created* the insomnia with which they are now trying to cope by using more alcohol.

The alcohol molecule is a neurotoxin that damages the parts of your brain that control sleep. Have you ever wondered why it is so difficult to sleep through the night when you've been drinking? Alcohol makes your brain move too quickly between its sleep states, simultaneously suppressing REM (rapid eye movement) sleep and creating night sweats and headaches (Stein and Friedmann 2005). Dreaming is a primary aspect of REM sleep, and having an adequate amount of this state of sleep is essential for the quality of your health and your mood. If you don't have enough REM sleep at night, you feel horrible and exhausted in the morning.

A man who feels miserable and has insomnia might tell himself, *I need a few drinks to fall asleep.* As he drinks, his anxiety is temporarily lessened; he becomes groggy and passes out. But the ethanol molecules don't go to sleep. They spend the night smashing against his highly stressed neurons, directly damaging his sleep cycles, and thus he wakes up exhausted with a headache and soaked sheets. The next day feels even worse than the day before, so he reaches for a drink that night, and the cycle repeats itself.

Drinking and severe depression don't mix. When you're severely depressed, you feel absolutely miserable. You are barely making it through the day, and sometimes you may even think about killing yourself. Your brain, your spirit, and your soul are under siege. Every time you consume alcohol, this depressant compound makes you feel much, much worse. And both you and I know we are probably not talking about drinking only a cold beer on a hot day. You probably drink more than that—a hell of a lot more. What you decide to do about your drinking is completely up to you, but please consider this information carefully.

If you decide to quit drinking. After reading about how alcohol affects sexual desire and sleep, you may be thinking about cutting back or even quitting drinking. But maybe you're stuck wondering about which of the many ways to cut back or to quit would work best for you. To begin to figure this out, I suggest you adopt an information-gathering perspective.

First, I recommend that you contact a mental health professional or an organization such as AA that specifically works with men who want to quit drinking. Meet with them and specifically ask what they have seen that works. Gather information, and bear in mind that it is likely that you will need to talk to a lot of different folks, some of whom you will not like nor feel like they understand what you are going through. But if you keep gathering information, you will eventually run into folks who do understand, and they may be able to help you. The more information you gather, the stronger you will become.

Approaching problems in life from an information-gathering perspective can be extraordinarily liberating. First, the process can take away the pressure you might feel to immediately make the right decision—for example, should you check into a rehab facility or join AA? Feeling pressured to make this kind of decision may seem to imply that your future is already decided, and if you do the wrong thing your fate will be sealed. This type of all-or-nothing catastrophic thinking will lead to paralysis. But if you tell yourself, *I am just going to*

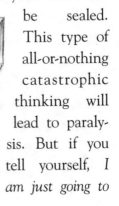

gather some more information by making a phone call, or by looking up something on the Internet, or by trying a single AA meeting, or by researching what kind of treatment my insurance may cover, you may find the motivation to move forward. This perspective works especially well when you feel stuck or resistant, or if you tend to procrastinate.

Second, once you determine a direction that seems like it might be helpful—be it counseling, 12-step meetings, rehab, or something else—continue to treat yourself as your own personal "research project." Let yourself try something, but just as an experiment in the beginning. See where the action takes you. Remind yourself that you are the one who is in control of this experiment, this test. If it is not working, you can try a different approach.

Pot and Your Severe Depression

What most fascinates me about pot is why it doesn't work better. How come its reported effects of euphoria and relaxation don't cure severe depression? I realize that I see a biased sample of clients in my office, but I have talked with many severely depressed men who smoke weed, and they are absolutely miserable. Some smoke pot on occasion, some on the weekends, and some every day, yet they all tell me that they are barely getting through the day and that their very existence is often unbearable.

Not only is marijuana extremely ineffective for treating severe depression, but it actually makes severe depression much worse. Why? Because it does three things.

First, the effect that the active ingredient in marijuana, or THC (tetrahydrocannabinol), has on the brain of a severely depressed person is very similar to that of the ethanol molecule.

THC initially reduces the subjective experience of anxiety by stimulating the brain cells to release the neurotransmitter dopamine (Leafscience 2018). Dopamine is intimately involved with the reward center in the brain, and as it is released, the person experiences the "high." As the chemical is metabolized, the neurotransmitters serotonin and GABA are impaired (Crippa et al. 2009), and the person experiences the inevitable rebound of depressive symptoms. The underlying anxiety and depression come rushing back, and the severe depression is stronger than ever.

As the saying goes, "Individual results may vary." Approximately 30 percent of pot users experience this intense anxiety immediately (Crippa et al. 2009), but these are usually not the ones who stick with it. Many men who smoke pot also drink. This is a problem for your brain because research has shown that alcohol causes THC to be absorbed faster into the blood plasma (AACC 2015). Essentially, many depressed men have found that drinking while smoking pot increases the speed at which those euphoric feelings arrive, but drinking alcohol *and* smoking pot is like doubling down on a longshot bet—the bet being that doubling the intoxicants will make the depression go away that much more quickly—and stay away.

Of course it returns, with a vengeance.

The second problem that a severely depressed man is going to have with pot is the amotivational syndrome that accompanies the feelings of relaxation. *Amotivational syndrome* means being unable to find the willpower to do things; in particular, pot makes it difficult to do things that delay immediate gratification, such as working on an unpleasant task that one has been avoiding, and instead encourages flipping on the TV and digging into a large bowl of ice cream. In other words, pot will make a severely depressed man who is already having the damnedest time motivating himself even more lethargic and lazy.

Lack of motivation is a primary symptom of depression. The Beast attacks your willpower. It understands very clearly that your willpower is essential to your command and control station, so that is one of the things it aims to take out in order to control you. From the Beast's perspective, nothing could be better than flooding your brain with a drug that makes you feel less motivated. If you already feel miserable, that your life is full of terrible problems, getting stoned is not going to get you off your butt. The Beast wants to decrease your motivation and willpower because it does not want you to engage in actions and behaviors that will reduce your stress and help you feel less depressed.

The Beast also knows that many of us deeply believe that motivation comes first and action second, because we have been trained to wait for the feeling of motivation before we do anything. This is a lie, because the brain doesn't actually work this way. It is action that produces motivation, not the other way around. The more we activate ourselves, the more motivation we will experience. The more your brain engages in a behavioral activity, the more willpower it will produce to continue that activity (Di Domenico and Ryan 2017).

But, you may be thinking, *I feel like crap and I just can't do anything.* Yes, I clearly understand how you might arrive at this conclusion, but keep in mind that this is the voice of the Beast. The Beast is desperately trying to get you to believe that you can't do anything without feeling motivated first.

Let's challenge this notion to see who is right. Start by taking a breath in through your nose and holding it for three seconds. Now slowly let it out through your mouth. Repeat this nine more times. Breathe in through your nose and out through your mouth. When you breathe in, expand your stomach. Focus on the sensation of the cooler air coming in through your nose and the warmer air passing out through your lips. When you are done, congratulate yourself. You have successfully tried deep meditative breathing. You motivated yourself to breathe deeper without waiting for a "feeling" to come along. The score between you and the Beast is now 1 to 0.

The third problem with pot and severe depression, and I believe this is the biggest problem with pot, is that it will separate you from other people. Yes, the THC chemical may give you the subjective experience that you are more connected to other people, but this is an illusion. The objective reality is that these other people are going to feel distanced from you. Other people cannot truly feel connected to you when you are stoned, because you are not interfacing with them; you are connected to the THC chemical. You won't be able to track their thoughts and feelings with integrity because you are absorbed in your own sensations.

Social isolation is another symptom of severe depression. The Beast wants you to feed yourself a chemical that increases your isolation. The fewer authentic connections you have with other people, the lonelier you will become. The deep canyon that exists between you and others is precisely what the Beast is after.

It is now legal to use marijuana and medical marijuana across a great deal of the United States. Many people who use pot use it in moderation, just as they use alcohol. But this book is not written for the vast majority of people; it is written for men like you who are wrestling with horrible, severe depression. I'm not asking you to consider the morality of pot; rather, I want you to consider the biochemical effects it has on your traumatized brain. Keep this image in mind as you consider marijuana use: If you are in the midst of a severe depression, it's as though there is a gash in your brain—that is, the neurochemistry that helps to regulate your mood has been impaired. This gash is part of why you feel so miserable. THC, the active ingredient in marijuana, will directly affect the neurotransmitters (serotonin and norepinephrine) that are intimately involved with how you experience your feelings (Fitzgerald 2013). The more THC in your brain, the more these neurotransmitters will be hammered, and the worse you will feel.

If you do decide to quit using pot. For many of the folks who successfully quit, the first thing they told me they did was throw out everything in their house directly connected to pot. And when they said "throw out," they meant it, as in flushing the weed down the toilet, smashing the bong, burning the rolling papers, and tossing the roach clips and pipes in the garbage, as opposed to just putting these things in a drawer where they would silently tempt them. Several people also said they deleted the contact info for their dealers. These folks weren't pretending that they didn't know where they could go to get more pot or paraphernalia, but the house purging went beyond a symbolic gesture. These people felt it was crucial to clean up their living space. Quitting anything is hard enough, and they didn't want any temptations in front of them.

Next, some of these folks told their close friends and family members that they were quitting, and that they were serious. They asked people whom they trusted for their support. This seemed to work best when they had people in their lives who could offer encouragement even if they had a relapse. In marriages or relationships in which both partners smoke and one partner is trying to quit, getting involved with Narcotics Anonymous (NA) proved helpful.

Many borrowed the strategy of taking things one day at a time directly from AA and NA. That is, they focused on just making it through each day. That's it. They remained focused on the moment at hand, believing the future would take care of itself.

Personally, I find this concept to be extremely valuable, and it can be applied to so many aspects of life. The only thing you have to focus on is today. You don't have to focus on tomorrow or the day after that. Just stay focused on the present. Worrying about whether you'll be smoking pot five years from now is overwhelming. It's much easier to focus on the day at hand. Remind yourself that at this moment, you are experiencing the trauma of severe depression, and at least for now you are concentrating on healing the wound in your brain. For this day, you are making the conscious decision not to flood your brain with chemicals like THC (pot) or ETOH (alcohol) that will make your depression much worse.

Some of my clients remarked that knowing what to expect regarding the initial symptoms of withdrawal helped them stay the course of quitting. Knowing that the symptoms were *temporary* was critical. Most physical symptoms, including increased body temperature and sweating, difficulty sleeping, and decreased appetite or nausea, peak within one to three days of quitting and completely subside within two weeks. Psychological symptoms, including feelings of anxiety and irritability, also subsided within a few weeks of quitting. Again, knowing that these symptoms were part of the withdrawal process, and that they would soon pass, helped many folks get through the quitting process.

A final strategy I'll offer, one I personally have had a lot of luck with when trying to change some aspect of my own behavior, is something I learned in my psychology training: the first step to change any behavior is to measure it.

How do you do this? Start by measuring the behavior you want to change before you start to change it. In terms of pot, just record how often you smoke it. Of course, if you choose this strategy, you have to be completely honest and record accurately each time you use. Recordings over a two-week period will give you a fairly accurate picture of your baseline usage. Once you have that baseline, you can then set a goal for reducing how much you use. The numbers don't lie and will help you to clearly see the direction you want to head in. For example, if you reduce your use by 25 percent a week, you will be clean in a month. If you decide to try this method, be sure to keep a record for the entire quitting process.

Other Drugs and Your Severe Depression

Alcohol and pot are the most common substances that severely depressed men use to try to feel better. There are, of course, many other legal prescriptions (particularly opioid painkillers such as oxycodone, Oxycontin, Fentanyl, Percocet) and illegal drugs (meth, cocaine, heroin) that people use to try to control how they feel. Your Beast is not picky. The initial high these drugs offer is always followed by an aching low that leaves one in despair, which is what your Beast is after. Abusing commonly prescribed antianxiety drugs creates the same effect. If your Beast has you consuming these illegal poisons or abusing legally prescribed drugs, I encourage you to attend a local NA meeting. Remember, if you do go to a meeting, you don't have to talk—you don't have to do anything. You are allowed to just sit and listen.

Saturated Fats and Sugar and Your Severe Depression

In addition to alcohol and drugs, saturated fats and sugar are specific compounds that cause your mood to plummet. Saturated fats are those that are generally solid at room temperature and are found in meat and dairy products. They are considered the unhealthy type of fat because, over time, they can clog your arteries and lead to a heart attack or stroke (Nettleton et al. 2017). They are found in nearly all junk food, and the Beast absolutely *loves* junk food. The more saturated fats and junk food you eat, the better it is for the Beast.

The Beast is begging you to stop by the closest drive thru and grab a cheeseburger and a large order of fries. In the morning it wants you to work your way through the dollar menu, starting with two bacon, egg, and cheese biscuits; and a coffee milkshake never hurts either. A meat lover's pizza would be great for lunch, and is this the night you can get twelve pieces of fried shrimp for $7.99? On and on it goes.

However, as problematic as saturated fats can be, added sugar is the one compound that most of us love that is really bad for the brain and depression. Added sugar are the sugars and syrups that are put into processed food such as high-fructose corn syrup. The average American consumes more than 152 pounds of added sugar every year, about one-third of it in the form of soda (NH DHHS 2014). Sugar has the same net effect on your brain as alcohol (NH DHHS 2014). The initial change in your mood is generally positive—or, more specifically, you experience instant gratification. You take a sip of ice-cold soda or a spoonful of that delicious chocolate ice cream, and your brain releases dopamine (Avena, Rada, and Hoebel 2008). If you are at all hungry, sugar tastes wonderful.

Millions of years of evolution have wired our brains to avidly seek out sugar and high-fat calories (Power and Schulkin 2009). We especially seek them out when we're stressed. The greater the stress, the more you will want to eat sugary desserts and fatty comfort food. But as with alcohol and drugs, while they may temporarily satisfy your hunger and boost your mood, before long you will experience the rebound. Your mood will plummet, your problems will appear worse, your motivation to adaptively solve your problems will decrease, and your sense of hopelessness will increase.

If your severe depression is laughing at me right now, thinking that I'm overblowing the importance of one's diet in relation to mood, ask yourself this: *When was the last time I felt down and found myself craving a large, fresh salad?* Does the Beast wake you up at dawn on Saturdays and fill your mind with worry that the farmers market is going to run out of kale if you don't get your butt out of bed? I didn't think so.

Fast food, junk food, comfort food—we love it all, as long as it is loaded with added sugar and saturated fat. If it comes in the form of bacon and processed cheese, all the better. The Beast also loves this food. It is the food many of us grew up with, the standard American diet, which is the daily diet for so many. But if only it worked to keep our brain happy. Just as with alcohol, it can be difficult to see and understand the relationship between consuming saturated fat and excess sugar and what happens to your mood. This is especially true of well-made comfort foods, the kind your mother or grandmother made, because these are often truly delicious, and don't easily fall into an obvious junk food category, like the food at your local drive thru.

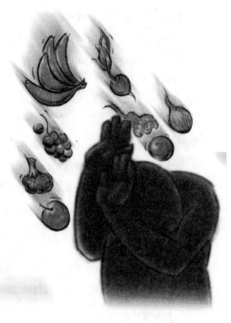

If you do decide to change your diet. So, what are you going to do? Again, that is up to you. Ideally, I would love for you to be able to say to yourself, *You know, at this moment I am dealing with severe depression. It is like a wound in my brain. Because I've got this gash, I am choosing to flood my brain with chemicals found in healthier foods. I am not saying I am going to do this forever, but*

at least for now and the next two months, this is what I am going to try.

While I do think it would be helpful for you to eat a lot more green vegetables during the next few months, I don't think a man has to become a strict vegan—that is, not eat anything that once had a set of eyes—to defeat the Beast. I don't think one should become a diet fanatic, because diets, which are often driven by perfectionism, typically end in failure. To me, the real issue with saturated fats and sugar seems to be one of balance, but finding this is easier said than done. You are currently experiencing severe depression. Your life is miserable. The Beast is telling you to feed it saturated fats and sugar. It does not want to wait, and it's demanding that you feed it NOW!

With that in mind, I have one simple recommendation: stop drinking your calories; more specifically, don't drink soda. The average twelve-ounce can of soda contains eleven teaspoons of sugar. Not allowing the Beast to flood your brain with this carbonated sugar water will help your brain heal from depression.

Electronic Media and Your Severe Depression

You may be surprised to learn that the same neurochemical pattern that underlies the effects of alcohol, pot, and excess fat and sugar also unfolds when you flood your brain with electronic media. Just as with those other "foods," the Beast wants you to consume as much electronic media—TV shows, movies, online videos, video games, Facebook posts, and so on—as possible. Or, to put it more succinctly, the Beast is desperately trying to turn you into a couch potato.

Why? The Beast wants you to be as passive as possible. *Don't move, sit still, and watch others live!* It wants you to observe the world from a safe distance. It does not want you to engage with other people. It does not want you to have meaningful relationships. Ideally, the Beast would have you stay on the sidelines and remain a passive spectator of your own life.

The more you avoid taking any action in life by passively watching an electronic screen, the stronger the Beast becomes. The passive consumption of media energizes it. Again, the issue is not whether you watch *some* TV, surf the Internet *for a while*, or play *a few* video games; it has to do with balance. Doing these things in moderation may not have a negative effect on your mood, whereas melting into the couch for hours on end does make the Beast feel a hell of a lot better.

Wrapping Up

The issue of what you feed the Beast can be reduced to quantity. The effects of alcohol, pot, excess sugar and fat, and media are dose dependent; the greater the dose, the greater the effect.

Yet when it comes to the severely depressed brain, the doses needed to start the depressed rebound state are significantly lower compared with a brain that isn't severely depressed. Remember, your brain has been traumatized with stress, so flooding it with these chemicals and couch-potato behaviors dramatically increases feelings of morbid depression. I keep hammering this issue because it's important.

I am sure that by now you recognize that while your depression is powerful and complicated, the tricks it uses are very simple: it tries very hard to take over your behavior and get you to do things that make it stronger. The more alcohol you drink, pot you smoke, sugar and fat you eat, and electronic media you consume, the stronger the Beast becomes, and the more depressed you feel.

The Beast is clever, and it knows that in order for it to be most effective, it has to wait for opportune moments to strike. These ideal moments are when your brain is under intense stress, such as when you are confronted with too many problems that you don't know how to cope with. Then it whispers in your ear, *Man, you need a break. You need to blow off some steam and relax, and I've got just the thing.* However, the "thing" the Beast wants you to consume or to do always leads to the same pattern in your brain: initial feelings of relaxation followed by a rebound of feeling even more miserable.

In my years of experience as a therapist, I've met countless men for whom this pattern comprises the essence of the behavioral, emotional, and physical syndrome that is severe depression. It is what transforms a depressed mood into severe depression. This pattern is why you are so miserable. Your Beast has you doing things that are making it stronger. It will trick you into flooding your brain with the depressant alcohol molecule, the demotivating THC compound in pot, or the mind-numbing effects of excess sugar and electronic screens.

You can change this pattern. You can alter your behavior and starve the Beast. You can stop feeling so miserable and helpless and start feeling better and more in control of your life. In case you think that feeling better only means *giving things up* or *not doing things* you enjoy, there are many positive things you *can* do that will interrupt the pattern that is worsening your severe depression. I'll discuss these in the next chapter.

Chapter 2

What Starves the Beast?

The way you behave determines how you will feel. While this may seem obvious, it bears repeating: the way you behave determines how you will feel. Why? Because behavior directly changes brain chemistry. Imagine, for example, you came upon a car that had a flat tire and quickly made the decision to pull over and lend a hand. You would immediately feel different than if you had decided to give the stranded driver the finger as you flew by. The moment-to-moment choices you make dramatically impact how you feel.

The chemicals involved in mood regulation are not just passively floating around in your brain; they are specifically directed and activated by the way you behave. This means that your behavior controls your feelings. Of course, most severely depressed men argue the opposite—that the way they feel dictates how they behave. In my practice I commonly hear things like "I am irritable and don't like to be around people, because I am miserably depressed and feel like crap." Or "I am exhausted and down; that is why I am drinking. I deserve a break. I deserve an escape." This is the voice of the Beast, and these are its lies. The Beast desperately wants you to believe that your depressed mood is always in control of your behavior. It doesn't want you to think that your behavior can positively impact how you feel.

A primary goal of this book is to teach you how to engage in specific behaviors that will flood your brain with positive chemicals. Now, a critical reader who has been immersed in the sciences might immediately point out that when it comes to the neurotransmitters in our brain, there really is no such thing as a "positive" or a "negative" chemical. In a literal sense, that is true. But I'm referring to a strategy when I use these terms: there are behaviors we can engage in that will help us to feel much better, just as there are behaviors we can do that result in us feeling much more depressed. Your Beast wants you to engage in those behaviors that deepen your sense of hopelessness. It loses energy when *you choose* to do behaviors that take care of your body, your spirit, and your need for deeper connection.

What are these Beast-starving behaviors? I'll start with the most direct way to change your mood: exercise.

Exercise: The Enemy of Severe Depression

Exercise changes brain chemistry for the better. If you can move, you can exercise. When it comes to severe depression, the goal of exercise is very simple: to make more of the neuro-chemicals in your brain that dramatically improve how you feel. The goal is not to build muscles, nor is it to lose weight. It is nice if those things happen, but they are not the real reason why I am suggesting you exercise. When you actively move your body, your brain produces more dopamine, serotonin, nor-epinephrine, and endorphins. These are the neurochemicals that are the foundation for your mood (Jenkins et al. 2016). As your brain manufactures more of them, you will begin to feel better. The way to get your brain to make more of these chemi-cals is to increase your cardiovascular activity (Thorén et al. 1990). Exercising for thirty to sixty minutes a day floods your brain with these positive, "feel-good," neurochemicals.

The specific type of exercise you choose does not matter, as long as you make it aerobic, which just means moving your body so that you are breathing a bit harder than normal, your heart is beating faster than it typically does, and you are on your way to breaking a sweat. You want to do this for thirty to sixty minutes a day at least four to five times a week. You can jog, cycle, swim, or play soccer or a pickup game of basketball. Just do something to get your heart moving faster than it nor-mally does. I am a big advocate of very slow running, because you don't need much equipment and you can do it by yourself, almost anywhere, in practically any kind of weather.

If I had a prescription pad and a man came to me with severe depression, this is exactly what I would write down: run slowly for thirty minutes a day, five times a week. While it is easy to tell someone to exercise, I know it is a lot harder to get oneself to do it. Many men struggle to find the motivation to run, in particular. I don't think that weather is the problem, nor is it getting ahold of a pair of comfortable sneakers; rather, it's the thought *Man, I hate running.* When I hear people say that, I think that this person has not yet discovered the art of *slow running.* That is, he thinks of running as something that is all or nothing—as an activity captured by the ridiculous phrase "No pain, no gain." People who repeat this phrase to themselves will often push themselves until they feel like they are about to throw up, but soon give up running altogether. What they don't realize is they don't have to push themselves so hard. They are allowed to run any way they want, including very, very slowly. Running very slowly and running fast are both powerful cardiovascular activities; either one spurs the brain to manufacture those feel-good neurochemicals. However, if you purposely allow yourself to run very slowly, I mean just jogging along at an easy, smooth, comfortable pace, you may find yourself not dreading it. And this might help get you out the door and taking that decisive first step, which is always the hardest step, but in the end is the only one that really matters.

Another way you might be able to motivate yourself to take that first step out the door is to remember this thought: *the Beast is afraid of sweat.* It never wants you to move because it does not want you to generate positive neurochemicals in your brain. As you flood your brain with endorphins, that horrible weight of severe depression begins to lighten. I am not saying that you are suddenly going to be cured if you jog around the block, nor are you guaranteed to get a runner's high every time you lace up your sneakers, but after you are done with your run and have taken a shower, you generally will feel a little bit better. And that little feeling, which typically lasts for six to eight hours after a run, is crucial to breaking the back of the Beast.

Exercise and the Activation of Your Genetic Makeup

You have approximately twenty thousand genes in your body (Gjevestad, Holven, and Ulven 2015). However, not all the genes in a cell are active. A gene can be activated or deactivated by diet and exercise. This is called *gene expression*, and it is the process by which genes use the information stored within them (as DNA) to make compounds like proteins. Proteins tell cells what to do, such as make more serotonin in the brain, which can dramatically help improve your mood. Exercise can directly turn on more than seven thousand of your genes (Booth, Chakravarthy, and Spangenburg 2002). Regular exercise has also been shown to alter the action of genes involved in the storage of fat and sugar, which then helps your body process these calories much more effectively (Rönn et al. 2013). As little as two hours of exercise a week, or thirty minutes of aerobic activity four days a week, can influence how many of your genes operate (Lindhom et al. 2014; Werner et al. 2008).

The bottom line is that more than 30 percent of your genetic makeup is dependent upon whether you chose to move your body. While each person's genetic makeup is determined by parents, that doesn't mean those genes necessarily determine destiny. A man has the ability to directly affect his own genetic makeup by what he chooses to do. If you make a decision to exercise, it will activate more than a third of your genes. Or, to put it another way, you have the power at this very moment to change the neurochemistry in your brain.

This is why it is so clearly the Beast of depression talking when a person says there is nothing he can do about how he feels. Science shows us this is simply not true. In your state of hopelessness, the Beast is roaring in your ear, *This is BS! There is nothing you can do. Maybe this works with other people, but it will not work with you.* If this is what you are hearing, then you know you are on the right track, because it means the Beast is frightened. You were never supposed to have this thought: *one-third of my genetic makeup can be impacted by whether I choose to sweat.* Sweating can change your life.

> **Do this to upset the Beast:** Write this on a piece of paper and stick it on your bathroom mirror: Each time I do a slow aerobic exercise for thirty minutes, I begin to turn on a third of my genes.

> **Do this to piss off your depression:** Slowly run to your car, get in, make sure the windows are closed, and yell these words as loudly as you can: "Exercise changes brain chemistry! If I move my body, I will feel less depressed!" Then slowly run back to whatever you were doing.

The Beast hates it when you initiate friendliness. Here is another direct strategy to upset your Beast: on your morning jog—or during your regular walks or however you choose to be active—make it a point to be the first person to yell out good morning or hello to each person you see. The goal is not to get the other person to respond in kind. Yes, it is nice when other people acknowledge you as well, but what matters is that you initiated contact.

I run on a country road each morning when most of the traffic is composed of people whizzing by on their way to work. For the longest time, I estimate that about 80 percent of the drivers gave me extra room as they passed by, whereas the other 20 percent did not offer me a clear berth. This infuriated me. So there I was, supposedly going for my soothing morning jog, but in reality I was working myself into a frenzy of anger because some of the drivers did not seem to acknowledge my presence. And, yes, on more than one occasion I found myself giving them the finger as I stared at their taillights.

This went on for quite some time. Then it occurred to me that perhaps I should take the advice I was giving my clients. Instead of focusing on what I could not change (the behavior of the drivers), maybe I should focus on what I *could* change (my own behavior). So I decided to end my futile war with the morning rush hour and instead become the morning greeter. I know this sounds ridiculous, but that is what I told myself. From then on, I offered *every single car* that passed me (I run toward oncoming traffic) a very conspicuous friendly wave. It didn't matter if the drivers slowed down, or if they acknowledged my presence by moving over a few feet. I waved at everyone.

Two things happened. The first was that most of the drivers started waving back. (Actually, on most days now almost every driver waves back. Many of them seem to recognize me, and quite a few honk their horn in greeting or flash their lights.) Second, I started feeling much better. I know that sounds strange, but I now feel like I have taken my power back and see myself as an established part of the community. It is almost like jogging through a small town where folks greet you by name. (I'm sure quite a few see me as the local eccentric, but as my brother has pointed out, every village needs an idiot.) Yes, of course there are still drivers who don't budge an inch, and my middle finger has not been retired for good, but this approach seems to be better for my mood than working myself up into a fury.

> **Do this to irritate the Beast:** Go outside now for a fast fifteen-minute walk and make it a point to wave or say hello to each person you see.

Depression hates it when people exercise as a group. Exercising by yourself is fine, but exercising with someone else is even better. Dr. James Blumenthal and his colleagues at Duke University showed that jogging three times a week for at least thirty minutes with a group of people treats depression as effectively as medication (Blumenthal, Smith, and Hoffmann 2012). Think about this for a second. If you can find a few people who will go for slow runs with you, and you do this three times a week for about four months, your neurochemistry will change in more positive ways than if you had spent thousands of dollars on the most advanced antidepressant medications ever invented.

Science has shown this to be true, but of course it would be difficult for a large pharmaceutical corporation to make money by just encouraging depressed folks to get together for a jog. The benefits of jogging don't end with improvement in your mood. You will soon see improvements in your cardiovascular system, your pulmonary system, your kidneys, your liver, how your body stores and metabolizes sugar and fats…and the list goes on and on (Awopetu 2014). But don't forget, if for any reason slow running is not your thing, you never have to do it. However, I encourage you to find an aerobic exercise that does work for you, and that you do that for at least thirty minutes a day, five times a week.

> **Do this to steal energy from the Beast:** Make a list of two to three guys who might possibly join you for slow runs. Contact each one and invite him to join your group. If they can all make it, great. If not, get out there anyway and let them know the invitation stands.

The Importance of a Decent Night's Sleep

I don't want to lecture you about how important it is to get a decent night's sleep. I know damn well you would love to have good sleep, but your depression is completely screwing it up. However, I do want to highlight the things that the Beast is getting you to do to make your sleep as bad as possible. And, because figuring out how to get better sleep is crucial to your healing process, I will offer specific suggestions for dramatically improving your sleep—thereby starving the Beast of the energy it needs to ruin your life.

You have learned that it's important to treat your severe depression with respect. You also need to treat your natural, essential need to get a decent night's sleep with great respect. Your mood relies upon quality sleep. In fact, forced sleep deprivation is classified as a form of torture. Your Beast will try to get you to torture yourself, by tricking you into doing things that ruin your ability to sleep.

The Beast will whisper in your ear that sleep is not all that important, that you don't have to take it seriously, and that there is nothing you have to do during the day to induce a good night's sleep. It will tell you not to worry if you don't get enough sleep, because you can always grab a cup of coffee or pick up a case of energy drink the next day. The Beast will tell you that it doesn't really matter how much sleep you get, because you can always make it up during the weekend.

These whispers are lies. Your Beast knows that getting a decent night's sleep is one of the primary building blocks your mood rests upon. You feel better after a good night's sleep because when you are sleeping your brain performs essential housecleaning and restores itself. During sleep, more cerebral spinal fluid is able to flow into your brain more quickly, helping to wash out excess toxins that build up during the day, such as fragments of beta-amyloids (NIH 2013). *Beta-amyloids* are tiny pieces of protein that can clump together, forming plaques that inhibit different parts of the brain from communicating with each other. These plaques have been implicated in the development of Alzheimer's disease. In addition, while you sleep your brain prunes excess cells and other microscopic parts that it no longer needs. Allowing your brain to sleep for seven to eight hours so it can clean itself out will help you feel much better the next day.

For the most part, Americans don't really think sleep is all that important. Our culture glorifies caffeine, among other chemicals, that we flood our brains with in order to wake up. I have an admission to make: I love coffee. I am currently "sober" from coffee, but I am a true "coffeeholic." When I was a young man I worked in a diner and I prided myself on drinking a pot a day. I drank coffee the way other men drink beer. I drank it with a vengeance. And just like an alcoholic discussing beer, I would say with pride, "Oh, no, this doesn't have any real effect on me." It wasn't until I was in my early forties and my sleep had gone to hell that I realized there was a connection between coffee and my insomnia.

A colleague had come to town, and I asked him if he wanted to grab a cup of coffee. But he said no, that he had stopped drinking coffee. I was stunned, because just a few years back this was something we had routinely done together. I asked him why he had done this bizarre thing, and he explained that since he had gotten himself off coffee he was the only person who didn't yawn at 9:00 a.m. staff meetings.

At that moment I suddenly got it. It was coffee that had been making him tired in the first place. Why? Well, I did some research to find out. When a person is addicted to caffeine, the brain doesn't fully wake up until it has been flooded with caffeine. The sensations of being exhausted and irritable until one has a cup of coffee are symptoms of caffeine addiction. It is the coffee itself that causes the exhaustion and irritation.

Caffeine does many different things to the brain, but there are two effects I want you to think about. The first is that caffeine significantly interferes with the sleep cycle. It does this by causing a rebound effect, which occurs approximately twelve hours after a person drinks his last cup. For example, if a man drinks his last cup of coffee at 11 a.m., then around 11 p.m., just as he should be getting more tired, he finds himself much more awake as the caffeine resurges through his brain. Second, when he finally does fall asleep, he ends up having impaired sleep stages because of the caffeine, so when he wakes up in the morning he has not gotten enough deep sleep (Shilo et al. 2002). This leads to feelings of irritation and exhaustion in the morning—his addicted brain crying out for more caffeine. The man then consumes more caffeine to wake up, and so the cycle continues.

So what if I am groggy in the morning? This doesn't really have anything to do with my depression. This is exactly the thought the Beast wants you to have. Remember, it is desperately trying to get you to believe there is no connection between what you flood your brain with and how lousy you feel. It wants you to believe that there is only a positive connection between consuming caffeine—as well as alcohol, sugar, and fats—and feeling less miserable. What it doesn't mention is that the addiction to caffeine significantly increases your feelings of irritability, because when your sleep is impaired your brain does not have enough time to clean itself of toxins, which, when left behind, make your mood plummet.

It is important to note that caffeine does not have the same effect on everyone. Some people metabolize the chemical much more quickly, so it doesn't seem to negatively impact their sleep cycle (Yang, Palmer, and de Wit, 2010). Unfortunately, I don't seem to be in that group, and if I start drinking coffee my sleep soon goes to hell. The question for you is, what is making it so hard for you to get a decent night's sleep? My guess is it has something to do with flooding your brain with caffeine, be it coffee, sweet tea, soda, or energy drinks.

To get better sleep, you need to first convince yourself that getting good sleep is really important—and you need to take this seriously and be willing to do things to make it happen. Second, you need to implement sleep strategies that will make you feel drowsy. Lack of drowsiness is another way of looking at insomnia. Perhaps you struggle with becoming sufficiently drowsy at the right time of night, or you wake up in the middle of the night and can't figure out how to fall back asleep. Below I offer suggestions specifically designed to help you induce the sensation of drowsiness in your brain. To help you solidify these suggestions in your own mind, it helps to think of your bedroom as a cave, a place that is cool, quiet, dark, and free of artificial light.

Stop watching TV or other electronic screens ninety minutes before going to bed. Of course, with our enormous

TVs and all of the other electronic screens—laptops, e-readers, tablets, cell phones, and so forth—in our lives, this has become a Herculean task. While our technological inventions have rapidly changed, the sleep architecture in our brain has remained the same. The way we get drowsy and begin to move from wakefulness into the sleep stages is that the pineal gland inside the brain produces a hormone called melatonin. As this floods into your brain you get that wonderful sleepy feeling. But if you start looking at an electronic screen, light comes into your brain that then triggers the *hypothalamus*. Your hypothalamus will then tell your pineal gland to stop secreting melatonin and you will no longer feel drowsy (Gooley et al. 2011). By not staring at an electronic screen approximately ninety minutes before you want to fall asleep, you allow your brain to start producing the chemicals it needs to fall asleep.

Do not bring your cell phone into your cave. This is a really important point, and some people may have a harder time with this than stopping drinking alcohol or coffee. I strongly encourage you not to bring your phone into your bedroom. Being awakened in the middle of a sleep cycle by an incoming text, notification, or email is waste of energy. When you are in the middle of a severe depression, you don't need your cell phone to interfere with your pineal gland.

> **Do this to make the Beast anxious:** Create a separate cave for your phone to sleep in at night. This could be the bathroom, the trunk of your car, or a shoebox. Now you have your cave and your phone has its own cave. Don't let it barge into your space.

Keep your cave cool. A central part of falling asleep occurs when our core temperature drops a few degrees (Okamoto-Mizuno and Mizuno 2012). To make sure your core temperature drops efficiently, keep your bedroom as cool as you can. Here are a couple of other tricks for lowering your temperature: Take a warm bath an hour before going to bed. The bath will increase your body temperature, but when you get out of the water it will suddenly drop. The sudden drop will stimulate your pineal gland to produce melatonin, which will then make you drowsy. Another trick is to wear socks to bed. Warm feet cause your core temperature to drop slightly, which will help make you drowsy.

Keep your cave dark. Make your bedroom as dark as possible. Light, even very small amounts, inhibits the production of melatonin in your pineal gland. I recommend getting rid of any clocks, night-lights, phones, or other devices that emit light. If outside light comes through your windows, install light-blocking shades. For those devices you have to have by your bedside, find ways to block their light as well. For example, throw a towel over your alarm clock or direct its light away from your eyes.

Keep your cave quiet. Make your bedroom as quiet as possible. I am a very light sleeper—so much so that one night a kitten walking across the carpet woke me up. However, I found a solution. To make my room quieter I make it a lot noisier with a white-noise machine, the sound of which masks other noises. You can buy stand-alone units at many stores, but you can also download free apps for your smartphone or tablet. I use the same app setting every night, and now my mind is conditioned to get tired to the sound of chirping crickets.

Here are some other things you can do that will help you sleep better:

- Break a sweat every day.

- When possible, get some direct sunlight for at least ten minutes each day.

- Don't take naps. Naps fool your brain into thinking it has already done all of its needed house cleaning chores, so it then resists getting drowsy when you try to go to bed at night.

- When you lie down, read something that is not interesting to you.

- Go to sleep and get up at the same time each day. The earlier the better. I know that getting out of bed when the alarm rings after you've had a horrible night's sleep is particularly difficult, especially when you finally got some decent sleep around 3:30 a.m., but doing so can be beneficial. If you are able to roll out of bed at the same time every morning (including on the weekends), your brain will be trained to become sleepy the same time every night, and you will soon start getting better quality sleep.

- If you wake up at night and can't fall back asleep, try progressive muscle relaxation, a process of methodically tensing and relaxing the muscles in your body. While lying in your dark cave, tense your scalp for three seconds. Then let it relax for five seconds. Now move to your forehead and tense that for three seconds, followed by five seconds of relaxation. Continue to move down your face, including your eyes, cheeks, tongue, mouth, jaw, chin, and neck. Tense each part of your face for three seconds, followed by five seconds of relaxation. Continue this process of tensing and relaxation down through each muscle of your body. If you reach your toes and you are still awake, just work your way back up your body.

Prescription Sleep Medications

You might be wondering about the role of sleeping pills and sleep quality. For a man in the midst of an awful, severe depression, it is very important to talk with your medical provider about what is happening with your sleep, such as if you are wrestling with insomnia. Be sure to tell him or her that you feel like crap and you are very, very depressed. That last sentence may sound stupid, but too many men see a doctor and describe various problems, such as insomnia or body aches, but never mention that they are also miserably depressed. Your doctor needs to know what is going on with your mood in order to find the right sleep medication for you.

Whether your provider prescribes a sleep aid, or you pick up something over the counter, bear in mind that sleeping pills are designed for relatively short-term use. Also, many of these medications have side effects and in some people may cause depression or worsen preexisting depression. It is crucial that you discuss this possibility with your doctor. You will also want to discuss potential interactions the medication might have with any antidepressants you are taking. Before you go the sleeping-medication route, consider utilizing the behavioral-sleep strategies I listed above. They can be just as effective as taking a pill, and all of them are safe for long-term use.

In conclusion, I strongly encourage you to start taking your sleep much more seriously. It might help to repeat these sentences to yourself: *Because sleep is the foundation for the quality of my mood, I am going to help my pineal gland produce melatonin by avoiding the lights from electronic screens at least ninety minutes before I go to bed. This way my brain will feel drowsy. I am also going to stop flooding my brain with chemicals, such as alcohol and caffeine, which interfere with my sleep architecture. This way my brain will be able to go to sleep and clean out its toxins.*

Severe Depression and the Way You Think

What happens to the way you think when you are in the midst of a severe depression? The Beast tricks you into using patterns of thinking that make your depression much worse. I visualize this impaired thinking as the stinking breath of the Beast, a fog that makes it very difficult to accurately see the problems that are causing you stress. It blinds you to the reality of your life by grossly distorting the way you think about your problems. In short, severe depression, your Beast, severely screws up the way you think about your problems.

The Beast's goal is to make you feel miserable, and it does this by *hijacking your thinking* so that everything in your life seems worse. And the more horrific your problems appear to you, the worse you will feel. The Beast wants you to feel as helpless as possible so you are convinced that you have absolutely no control—over your mood, over the problems you are facing, or over your future. It whispers in your ear that you are an utter failure, that nothing you do makes any difference, that your life will always be horrible. This is all a lie.

Depression and Cognitive Distortions

How does the Beast hijack your thinking? How does it distort reality and make you feel worse? The Beast does this with cognitive distortions. Originally described by Drs. Albert Ellis and Aaron Beck in the 1950s and '60s, *cognitive distortions* are irrational thinking styles that don't include all the data present in one's life (Gaudiano 2008). When people focus solely on negative data and purposely overlook positive information or positive interpretations of what is happening, they are experiencing a cognitive distortion.

For example, imagine you sneeze and say to yourself, *I must have a cold. No, wait, it must be pneumonia. Damn, I am going to die tonight!* This is a distorted way of viewing an experience (the original sneeze) called *catastrophizing*.

Here is another example: A man says to himself, *My boss didn't say hello to me. He hates me. He is probably going to fire me this afternoon. We will lose the house. My family will leave me. I am going to be on the street. I am a complete failure. My life is over.* This example includes the cognitive distortions of *catastrophizing* (predicting the worst possible outcome) and *fortune telling* (predicting a negative, catastrophic event in the future based on inadequate data).

If these examples seem unrealistic, that is because they are. The cognitive distortions that underlie the thinking patterns of severe depression—including yours—are always unrealistic. Because these thinking patterns are based on illogical reasoning, the person leaves out any possible positive or even neutral interpretations of the original event, so the conclusion the person draws ends up making him feel worse.

The fog of your severe depression may seem all-encompassing. You are miserable and feel like nothing is ever going to change. At this very moment you may feel hopeless. Is the Beast whispering in your ear, *Cognitive distortions? Illogical thinking styles? What the hell! I told you he has no idea what you are going through.* And in that respect the Beast is right. I don't know the specific details of what you are going through, but I do know that I can teach you how to cut through the haze of your depression. I do know that it is possible for you to learn a straightforward way to analyze your problems much more effectively.

You can learn to analyze your problems in a much clearer light using what's called cognitive behavioral therapy (CBT), a step-by-step method for changing thinking. Quickly identifying and actively challenging the cognitive distortions your Beast is flooding your mind with is how you can become your own lighthouse in the rough seas of depression. Yet, it is important to remember that just because you learn to identify and talk back to your cognitive distortions does not mean that your problems will go away. But the more you practice CBT, the more your Beast will suffer. It will lose energy. Your mood will change, and you will feel better.

Starving the Beast with CBT

Before I go any further, I have to admit that when I first encountered CBT I had a very negative reaction. Actually, I had more than a negative reaction; I hated it. I thought CBT was complete BS. To me, it seemed that therapists were telling depressed people that all they needed to do was "think positive" and everything was going to be all right. Every time I read about CBT, I would hear "Always Look on the Bright Side of Life" from *Monty Python's Life of Brian* playing in my mind, as in *Don't worry about your problems; just cheer up and everything will be fine.* Basically, CBT came across to me as another way to blame people for their own depression and kick them when they were down. I mean, what could be easier than telling someone who is going through living hell that all they need to feel better is just to restructure their thinking?

Yet as I spent more time listening to men who were in the middle of terrible depressions, I began to see CBT differently. It occurred to me that the strength of CBT is not so much its ability to make us feel better when we are going through horror; rather, it's that CBT can show us how we really can—and do—use our thinking styles to make ourselves feel so much worse.

For example, imagine you are stuck behind a slow-moving car. The driver seems to be braking for no reason. If you thought to yourself, *I bet this guy's texting. That asshole is trying to slow me down on purpose,* how would you feel? Most likely you would be pissed off and possibly generating some road rage. Now imagine the same scene, but this time you think to yourself, *That is my daughter, who is just learning to drive. I know she is nervous, but she is trying her best. She is a good kid. She will get it soon.* Now how would you feel? Concerned? Maybe. But inflamed by road rage? I don't think so. So, the bottom line of CBT is this: how you *think* about a problem will determine how you will *feel* about the problem.

Consider another example: If you tell yourself that you have always been an awful person in every respect, that no one will ever love you, and that your future will be filled with cease-less misery, you will soon feel worse. The opposite would be to tell yourself that there are parts of yourself that are okay and other parts you are working on; that you have had connections with people who are very meaningful to you; and though the future may be unknown, chances are there are some extraordi-nary experiences waiting for you. This thinking may provide a glimmer of hope.

The first step in practicing CBT is to remind yourself that how you think about a problem will contribute to how you feel about that problem. The second is to consciously step back from your mind and examine your thinking. You do this by asking yourself if your thinking is accurate. An easy way to do this is to say these lines out loud: "Because I am severely depression and dealing with real problems, I want to determine whether I am thinking about my problems accurately in this moment, or if my severe depression is dis-torting the way I view them. Is the Beast making my problems look much worse than they really are?"

Problems   PROBLEMS

Cognitive Distortion's Most Deadly Mind Tricks

In order to challenge the cognitive distortions with which the Beast envelops your mind, you will need to train yourself to recognize them. Although we are strangers, and I have never had the chance to speak with you, I'll bet the three mind tricks of cognitive distortion—overgeneralizing, catastrophizing, and black-or-white thinking—are deeply embedded in the way you think about the problems in your life.

Overgeneralizing. This distortion occurs when you draw a conclusion based on limited data while simultaneously ignoring positive data that do not support that conclusion. Overgeneralization is one of my go-to mind tricks that I regularly use on myself. A good example occurred while I wrote this very section on cognitive distortions. Throughout this book I am striving to make psychological ideas accessible. In the midst of your pain I want these dry academic ideas to seem as real and alive as possible. As I struggled to describe and explain the mind trick of overgeneralization, I started thinking that I had screwed up. Thoughts went through my head: *Maybe I can't write a book on severe depression. Who the hell is going to listen to me anyway? I should just admit I am a complete failure as a writer.*

These overgeneralized thoughts do not describe all the data; they are distortions of reality that specifically leave out positive pieces of information. The truth is, I didn't fail. Even though this section was difficult to write, I did finish it. And even if this book does not help all readers, that won't mean that I, Jonas, am a failure as a writer. Conversely, if you, the reader, don't get much out of this discussion about cognitive distortions, so what? Not everything applies to everyone. It certainly does not mean that you have failed. This is just one small section of the book, and there are other parts that may speak to you. The amazing thing is that you have made it this far, and considering how much pain you are in, that is a miracle in itself.

To grapple with the sly mind trick of overgeneralization, try to take a step back from your own thinking. Ask yourself, *Am I using the mind trick of overgeneralization? Am I telling myself only negative things that just don't hold up under scrutiny? Is it possible that at this very moment the Beast is getting me to overlook positive data because it wants me to feel as crappy as possible?*

The best way to explore these questions is with a piece of paper. At the top of the paper write down the negative thought you are having. Using the example of myself wrestling with getting this section done, I would write something like "I am a complete failure as a writer because I am struggling to get this section done." Now draw a straight line down the center of the paper. On the left side of the line list all the pieces of data that appear to support the original thought. Here I might write something like this:

I can't figure out what to say.

I haven't finished writing the section.

A real writer would not have a problem with this.

Then on the right side of the paper, write down all of the pieces of data that do not appear to support the original thought—that is, write down all the positive things you have done that the Beast is desperately trying to get you to ignore. You may have to force your mind to slow down and search for examples. It is important to remember that seemingly very small things do count and should be listed. So here I might write statements like this:

I may not feel that I've come up with the perfect way to express this particular idea, but I have written a few paragraphs.

I have already successfully written many other sections of the book.

I am not watching TV. I have the computer open and I am continuing to work on this section.

I've jotted down two notes, which really means I am on my way to completing this difficult section.

Once you have finished, take a step back and look over all the negative and positive data. Finally, ask yourself, *Does my original thought still stand?* In this case, I would ask myself, *Am I, Jonas, a complete failure as a writer because I am struggling with one small section of this book?* And when you look at it that way, by using a piece of paper to force your mind to include positive bits of data, the original negative statement doesn't stand and clearly looks like what it always was: a distorted overgeneralization.

Catastrophizing. This distortion is an exaggeration of a negative event. The smallest bad event is immediately transformed into an insurmountable mountain. Minor setbacks become death itself. The Beast whispers in your ear, *This is your fault, and it's the end of your F***ing world.* The only scenario the Beast wants you to believe is the worst case. It will lie to you and try to convince you that everyone else is afraid to speak the truth, and that you are the only one being a realist. What your Beast doesn't tell you is to think about alternative explanations: where you could then see that the stressful event you have run into is actually quite minor and you already have the ability to cope with it. It will never encourage you to consider some of the positive data that are right in front of you.

The Beast wants you to think catastrophic thoughts because they activate your autonomic nervous system. This is part of the system that floods your brain with adrenaline when you encounter dangerous situations so that you are primed for flight or to fight. While a racing heart is good if you are about to go into battle, or if you need to get the hell out of the way of a speeding bus, it doesn't help you to slow down and think. A shot of adrenaline does not help you conceive of positive interpretations. And this is what the Beast is after: it wants your brain to be flooded with adrenaline so that you cannot think slowly and purposely identify positive things about your own behavior or the stressful situation you're dealing with. The more it can convince you that you are facing a catastrophe and you are doomed, the more depressed you will feel.

Imagine that on a Friday afternoon your supervisor sends you a message saying that he wants to meet with you at 9 a.m. on Monday, and you immediately think, *That's it. I'm going to get fired. We won't be able to pay the mortgage. My wife is going to leave me. I'm never going to see my kids again. My life is over.* This is an example of catastrophic thinking. While you don't actually know what is going to happen at the meeting on Monday, you have reached the worst possible conclusions while ignoring other possible scenarios.

You can immobilize catastrophic thoughts with a pen and blank piece of paper. On top of the paper write down your catastrophic thoughts. For this example, I would write, "I am going to get fired. We are going to lose the house. My wife will leave me and I will never again see my kids. My life is over." Now draw a line down the center of the paper. On the left side write down the data that appear to support the negative catastrophic thoughts:

I knew he was going to fire me when he didn't say hello to me last Tuesday.

If I lose my job, I don't know what I am going to do.

My wife and I have been arguing a lot lately about money. If I lose my job, she'll take the kids and leave.

Then on the right side of the page write down every positive and neutral interpretation of the event you can think of:

My supervisor asked me to meet with him in the past, and each time it was to go over the sales report.

It is never easy for my wife and I to talk about money. Sometimes we argue, but a lot of times we don't. Both of us have had different jobs in the past, so even if this job comes to an end it doesn't mean my marriage is over.

The truth is, I just don't know what is going to happen on Monday. I will talk with my wife about it and tell her I am worried, but my life is not going to be over no matter what happens.

Remember, the goal of this exercise is not to try and pretend that something bad may not happen. Rather the aim is to try and slow down the adrenaline that is pumping through your body so you can think straight. Catastrophizing makes your mind go into a fight-or-flight mode. When your brain is preparing to flee or fight, it has a hard time taking in positive data. In the example I provided, while it is of course possible that the man's supervisor will fire him on Monday, it is much more likely that he simply wants to go over the latest sales reports. Remember, the more catastrophic thoughts the Beast can get you to believe and ruminate over, the less able you will be to see the full picture, and the happier the Beast will be.

Black-or-white thinking. This is all-or-nothing thinking. It is a cognitive distortion in which the Beast convinces your mind that there are no gray areas. Things are completely one way or the other. That's it; there is nothing else. Black-or-white thinking is particularly in control of your mind when you make negative statements about yourself: You are either lazy or you are not. You are either a failure or you are not. You are either an asshole or you are not. There is no gray area in any of these thoughts. And precisely because it is an absolute statement, it is a lie. These character assassinations purposely ignore positive aspects of your being. They are distortions of reality. Struggling with getting yourself motivated when you are severely depressed is not the same thing as being lazy. Not completing a task when you are having difficulty concentrating does not mean you are a failure. Feeling irritable and miserable when you are exhausted does not mean you are an asshole. What all these things mean is that you are depressed.

When you are stressed, take a step back and ask yourself, *Am I using black-or-white thinking? Is the Beast playing a mind trick and getting me to ignore gray areas? Are these absolute negative statements that I am making about myself absolutely true, or am I ignoring positive information?*

In my practice I regularly hear the phrase "I'm a complete failure." This common example of black-or-white thinking often comes out when a client is talking about something that has not gone well in his life, such as a problem at work, or a frustrating encounter he had with someone else, especially if he felt rejected. The word "failure" is stated as an absolute, and it typically is meant to cover everything he has done in the past, what is going on now in the present, as well as everything he might do in the future.

Once again, the pen-and-paper technique is the way to break apart black-or-white thinking. Start by putting the original, absolute negative statement on top. Evidence that appears to support it goes on the left:

Well, I felt like a failure, and that is the only thing that really mattered.

I didn't get what I wanted.

You don't know me. I always screw everything up.

When you are ready to do the right side of the page, where examples of positive data go, first remind yourself of the color gray. There are many shades of gray between black and white, just as there are lots of conclusions to be drawn that fall between negative and positive absolutes. Your job is to not only list the positive pieces of data that do not support the original statement, but also identify gray areas:

Yeah, I may not be a good match for that particular person, but I can name two other times when I was not rejected.

I can name a specific time when I got exactly what I wanted. Actually, I can name several times when that happened.

At this very moment I am trying to come up with some positive things I have done, and that in itself is positive.

The more the Beast screws up your perceptions and gets you to use these distorted thinking styles, the more depressed you will feel. Yet no matter how lousy you feel, no matter how depressed you are, you do have the ability to change the cognitive style you use to think about your problems. When you change your thinking style, an extraordinary thing happens in your brain.

The physical structures that are involved with both depression and anxiety begin to change. Researchers at Linköping University in Sweden used CBT with patients who suffered from anxiety and depression. After nine weeks of treatment, the amygdala, which is a part of the brain that processes anxiety, reduced in volume and activity (Linköping Universitet 2016). That you can use CBT to not only feel better but also to change parts of your brain is a powerful scientific fact to smack the Beast upside the head with.

Always remind yourself that the Beast is trying hard to make you more depressed by making your problems appear much worse than they are. The Beast wants you to think only about the negatives in almost every situation. It actively hunts for negative information and drools every time it can come up with something, *especially* self-criticism or judgment (that is, *I'm worthless… I'm an utter failure.*).

But your depression does not stop there. It also purposefully ignores positive information. The Beast hates positive information, and it especially hates any small good things you can say about yourself!

Now say this out loud: "The Beast gets stronger by looking for the worst in every situation. The more negative pieces of information my

depression can find, the stronger it grows." If your Beast is whispering in your ear that there is nothing positive you can say about yourself because you are a complete failure, loser, and so on, tell it that you know, for certain, that you are *really good* at emotionally beating the crap out of yourself.

Once you begin to monitor your thoughts, you will notice how often you are playing negative and self-demeaning "tapes" in your mind, and how often you disregard evidence to the contrary. If you remember anything from this section, it should be this specific trick: Once you identify a negative thought, grab hold of it and slap it down on top of a blank piece of paper. Draw a line down the center of the paper. On the left side write down the pieces of negative data that seem to support the thought, and on the right side all the pieces of positive data that do not support it. When working on the right side of the page, don't forget to purposely slow your mind down and include every possible piece of positive data you can find, especially that which seems really small and unimportant. The key to this whole exercise is to go through the process of writing down the thought and listing the pros and cons. I am not saying that with a good amount of practice you won't be able to just do this in your mind, but there is something about the physical process of writing that makes a crucial difference and directly targets the neurochemistry that feeds the Beast.

CHALLENGE THE LANGUAGE OF YOUR BEAST

Does the Beast yell in your ear, *This ALWAYS happens to me!* if another driver cuts you off? Does the Beast shout, *This happens EVERY time! Every damn time!* when you hit a red light while running late? The words "always" and "every" indicate that these experiences are absolutes that happen every time you drive in traffic or encounter a stoplight. Their use alone means that whatever the Beast is telling you is factually wrong. The statements are lies. You don't *always* get cut off in traffic, nor do you encounter a red light *every* time you drive.

The Beast loves to use words that are categorized as absolutes, such as "all," "every," and "each," because they are based on the cognitive distortion of black-or-white thinking. The Beast tries very hard to get you to speak to yourself using these words. It cringes if you use qualifiers or words based in the gray areas, such as "some," "sometimes," or "occasionally."

At this moment you may be wondering, *Why the hell does it matter what words I say to myself when I am stopped at a red light?* That is a great question. The Beast does not want you to see how it is subtly influencing your mind. It does not want you to see that by getting you to think in absolutes, it is getting you to purposefully ignore all the times that something bad did *not* happen to you. This is what the Beast is really after: it is training you to ignore positive information. The more it gets you to think in absolutes, using words such as "always," "every," "all," and "never," the more depressed you will feel.

Here's a trick I suggest to my clients: When you hear yourself use a word that is an absolute, circle it in your mind using an imaginary red marker. This act will remind you that the absolute is the voice of the Beast, and whatever it is saying is not based on reality. It is a cognitive distortion the Beast is using so you will ignore positive information. It is a mind trick intended to make you feel worse about yourself.

Avoidance, Procrastination, and Perfectionism

In the first chapter I discussed how the Beast turns your stressed-out, lousy feelings into severe depression in which you end up in a state of despair and just barely hanging on. I explored extensively the sneaky things the Beast tempts you to flood your brain with, such as alcohol, pot, electronic media, and crappy food, and how the temporary relief these mind-numbing things offer only sets the stage for your depression to rebound harder. Now I want to show you the behaviors the Beast gets you to do in order to maintain your severe depression. And, most important, I want to teach you techniques to break those behaviors.

The Beast will do anything it can to get you to avoid dealing with your problems. It knows, of course, that the longer you avoid dealing with your problems, the worse they generally become, and the worse they become, the more you are going to worry about them. Remember, the Beast's ultimate goal is for you to remain as passive as possible, so it can grow stronger. I am not just talking about lying on your bed. I am talking about all the things you do to avoid directly confronting your problems. Severe depression is like a tar pit hidden by thick fog. As you try to walk forward, barely able to see where you are going, the ooze sucks you down. It is so exhausting to move that you say to yourself, *I am just going to stay still—as still as I can be. I'll numb myself with TV, with video games, with the phone, with beer, with weed. I'll numb myself with crap— anything I can find. As long as I don't move, I will be okay.*

The Beast uses a variety of techniques to get you to avoid your problems. One of the most powerful is *procrastination*—that is, putting things off "until tomorrow." The Beast loves for you to procrastinate because the longer you delay doing the thing you feel like you need to do, the more you are going to worry and feel bad about yourself, and the stronger it will get. I am not talking about putting off things that you don't really care about, such as those tasks on someone else's to-do list. These are not things you will worry about delaying or not completing. The other person may say that you are procrastinating, but really you are passively avoiding his or her agenda. I'm talking about things you think you need to do. If you procrastinate with these, your brain is going to worry about them, and the Beast will feed off this worry. In order to get you to procrastinate, the Beast floods your mind with two simple but extremely powerful cognitive distortions to justify your behavior: all-or-nothing thinking and perfectionism.

With all-or-nothing thinking, the Beast convinces you that attempting to deal with a major problem in life means you have to deal with it 100 percent. You have to completely resolve it. The Beast uses this cognitive distortion because it knows damn well that the very thought of having to *completely* deal with any problem feels *completely* overwhelming. Thus, the chances of you procrastinating and avoiding the problem are awfully high.

To break free of this all-or-nothing Beast mind trick, tell yourself that you have the right to do just a little bit with regard to any of your problems. I call this the "little bit" strategy. I had a client who felt that his life was out of control because his desk was covered with papers—personal papers, tax forms, business letters, bills, files, and so forth. He had lived with this clutter for years and felt horribly depressed, believing he was "lazy" and "undisciplined." The very thought of even attempting to organize his desk exhausted him. The more he avoided directly approaching this stressor, the more miserable he became.

> **Do this to steal energy from the Beast:** Write down the very smallest thing you could do to solve just one of your problems. The smaller and more specific the behavior is, the better.

It had not occurred to him that there was no law that dictated he had to clean his desk all at once. Once he started to consider that he was allowed to approach this problem one small bit at a time, he went to Sears and bought an egg timer. (This happened in the days before cell phones.) He set the egg timer for 4 minutes and 53 seconds and started working on one corner of his desk. (He told me that he chose the odd time because working on his desk for 5 minutes seemed overwhelming.) It took him about 11 days to get his desktop cleaned off—less than 54 minutes; however, I wouldn't be surprised if he didn't "cheat" on occasion and go over his allotted 293 seconds. Even so, it likely took him only a few hours total.

The story doesn't stop with the cluttered desk, because he started using the egg timer to deal with other problems in his life, including having difficult conversations with his ex-wife, cleaning out his packed garage, updating his resume, and sitting quietly at the back of an AA meeting. He wasn't able to *completely* resolve *every* conflict he had with his ex-wife, or all the problems he had with alcohol, but he said the egg-timer trick made him feel that he was finally making progress, which led him to have a greater sense of control over his life. The Beast's procrastination technique was strong, but his egg timer was stronger.

The second mind trick the Beast uses to get you to procrastinate and avoid dealing with your problems is perfectionism. Perfectionism is the Beast's religion. I call this cognitive distortion the *religion* of perfectionism because so many people believe it is their job to always do everything exactly right. Then, when they don't do something perfectly, they beat themselves up as though they have committed some unforgivable sin. None of us is perfect, so this mind trick allows the Beast to launch its scorched-earth campaign of self-criticism. The more it gets you to humiliate yourself with self-criticism for not doing something perfect, the lousier you will feel.

When you are part of the congregation of the religion of perfectionism, the Beast has you convinced that you cannot do anything unless you are going to do it *perfectly*. In this religion you are not allowed to stop drinking unless you are going to do it *perfectly*. You are not allowed to exercise unless you are going to do it *perfectly*. You are not allowed to read this book unless you are going to do everything I suggest perfectly! This is the sly voice of the Beast. It knows damn well that if you believe for even half a second that you must do a task perfectly, you are less likely to attempt it, which leads us back to avoidance. However, some of us will still try to do things perfectly, and this isn't good either. Whether it's trying to perfectly clean up a desk, to perfectly jog, or to perfectly say all the right things during a conversation, striving for perfection in itself is bound to fail, because no one is perfect. This "failure" leads to self-loathing and replaying the self-criticism tape, which gives the Beast enormous amounts of energy. And that is exactly what your Beast is after. It wants you to avoid doing things so you end up hating yourself. The more you feel you must do things perfectly, the more you will avoid, and the stronger it grows.

In order to counter this cognitive distortion, I strongly recommend that you consciously try to be as imperfect as possible. Go for a jog and start walking halfway through; start cleaning up your desk but stop after forty-seven seconds; read this book again from the beginning, but this time only look at the illustrations. The point is that you are allowed to do things imperfectly, and the more you practice this skill, the less depressed you will feel.

> Write down one thing you are procrastinating doing. Now write down one specific way you could get this thing done—imperfectly. The more imperfect, the better.

> A classic CBT technique to break perfectionism is called thinking in percentages. Instead of telling yourself *I failed* (an all-or-nothing statement), tell yourself *I did 67 percent of what I wanted*, or *I am 51 percent of the way there*.

What if you can't find the motivation to fight all-or-nothing thinking or perfectionism? Recently, a client said to me, "I am waiting for motivation." He has been waiting for most of his adult life. I guess you could say he is very patient—maybe a bit too patient. Unless he takes drastic measures, he will most likely be saying the same thing next month, next year, next decade. For now, he waits and waits. The motivation doesn't seem to come.

The bad news is that the motivation he is waiting for is likely to never come. Why? Because he is violating the law of motivation by waiting for the *feeling* of motivation to arise in his gut, at which point he will get out there and "act."

The law of motivation is simple: action produces motivation. It is the "doing" of a behavior that creates the feeling of motivation (Koob 1996). We act, and then we experience increased motivation. *But I just don't want to do it.* That, of course, is not just the whiny, procrastinating voice of depression but the voice of thousands of chromosomes that have been deactivated by disuse. *I don't want to get off the couch. I don't want to turn off the TV. Don't move me. Don't touch me.*

So what do you do to jump-start motivation? First, I strongly suggest that you think of the behavior, task, or chore that you don't want to do, and then break it into the smallest bits you can think of. Be sure to make each "bit" a doable behavior that is as specific and as small as possible. Second, borrow that timing technique I mentioned earlier, and do the small behavior for 4 minutes and 53 seconds. If you decide to try this unusual motivation technique, please follow this one very important rule: at the end of 4 minutes and 53 seconds, you have to stop. Don't do it for 4 minutes and 54 seconds, or for 5 minutes. You should stop completely at 4 minutes and 53 seconds.

But this is ridiculous, the Beast may be saying. *I can't get it done in 4 minutes and 53 seconds. I can't get anything done in that short of a time frame.* Yes, this is probably true. It may take you longer than 4 minutes and 53 seconds to finish the behavior you're avoiding. But it probably won't take you longer than 4 minutes and 53 seconds to start it. In addition, by starting the process, your brain will create neurotransmitters such as dopamine, which underlies the feeling of motivation, and your motivation to engage in the behavior will increase (Grassian 2006).

After you have completed 4 minutes and 53 seconds, "rest" for the same amount of time, and then make a decision. Would you like to continue to round two or three? If you say yes to yourself, go for it, but remember that each round should be no longer than 4 minutes and 53 seconds.

A weapon to use against both perfectionism and procrastination is to break the task you don't want to do into small bits. If the thought of doing that small bit still seems horrible, then you haven't made the bit small enough. I encourage you to make the bits so small that the thought of doing one makes you laugh it's so easy.

Don't forget that even if you break the thing you need to do into tiny bits, your Beast hasn't disappeared and will still do everything it can to get you to procrastinate doing even the small bits. It will dangle right in front of you activities that seem much less awful. For example, it will get you to suddenly remember that your favorite show is about to start, or you will realize that you haven't checked your phone in the last six minutes, or it will remind you about that ice cream in the back of your freezer which you must eat right now.

At the same time the Beast is tempting you away from your tiny task, it will flood your mind with these three thoughts:

1. *The thing you are about to do is absolutely miserable.*

2. *You will never be able to do it.*

3. *If you try doing it, you must do it perfectly.*

Talk back to the Beast:

1. You have experienced much more miserable times in the past, and getting yourself to do this one tiny thing is not going to break you.

2. You will be able to do it, and you are already 51 percent of the way there because you have already starting thinking about it.

3. You don't have to do it perfectly. In fact, you are purposely going to try and do it imperfectly.

Another powerful strategy to beat both procrastination and perfectionism involves going after shame. Shame happens when the Beast whispers in your ear that you have violated some external rule, such as inadvertently walking around with your fly open or being a klutz and tripping over a curb in front of a crowd, and it convinces you that everybody else knows about this rule and they are now looking down at you. To get you to avoid doing something, the Beast will tell you that you are going to be shamed unless you do that thing perfectly, which then leads to the cycle of procrastination.

A great way to attack shame is to repeat to yourself this wonderful phrase: *It's none of your damn business what other people think of you!* I regularly say this to myself to break apart my own fear that other people are judging me.

As I have gotten older, at times I have felt very embarrassed to let other people see how slowly I run. Although I can remind myself that it is good that I am out there running at all, another voice is looking at my shadow and mocking me for how slowly

I am moving. When I am already feeling down, that mocking voice becomes very loud. It makes me think that the drivers whizzing by are actually looking at me and thinking to themselves, *What an idiot. That guy is barely shuffling.* However, when I remember to tell myself *It's none of your damn business what other people think of you!* I feel reenergized.

Worrying what other people think of me is basically like trying to control their thoughts. It is exhausting, not to mention impossible. More important, I also believe that everyone has a fundamental right to their own opinion, even if it's a thought or opinion about me that I do not like. When I start to feel shame, I find that actively reminding myself that people have the right to not like what I say or do allows me to stop worrying about what anyone else thinks about me. Because at the end of the day, it's their right and none of my business. With this in mind, I can let go of any shame I might be feeling, and instead focus on what I am doing.

While I encourage you to try this shame busting technique, it does not seem to last all day. My experience has been it lasts for about 3 minutes, before the worry starts creeping back in and I have to repeat the phrase, *It's none of your damn business what other people think of you.*

Write down one specific act that you want to do but are afraid of feeling shame for doing. Now repeat this phrase: "It's none of your damn business what other people think of you."

In conclusion, the Beast will do everything it can to get you to avoid dealing with the problems that cause stress in your life. It will try to convert you to the religion of perfectionism because it knows that the more you believe you have to do something perfectly, the less motivated you'll be to do it. The key to attacking the Beast's procrastination strategy is to break tasks into very small pieces. Then, set a timer and allow yourself to do one small bit at a time. Each time you do this the Beast loses energy, and you will feel less depressed.

Chapter 3

Interpersonal Relationships

The heartbeat of severe depression can be found in what is *not* happening between you and others.

If asked to name the feeling that underlies severe depression, I would say it is loneliness. Yes, the severely depressed men who come into my office express tremendous anger, which they direct back toward themselves. And, yes, these men engage in all sorts of behaviors that make their depression much worse. But what really seems to define them as a group is how intensely disconnected from other people they feel. They live in a world of isolated pain, and they feel very much alone. This includes both single men and men in relationships. Often the men who are in disconnected marriages feel the worst, because living with someone you are supposed to feel close to but don't can be extremely painful.

Loneliness doesn't stem from how popular someone says they are, how many virtual friends and followers they have on social media, nor even how many people they know. When it comes to being severely depressed, how lonely a man feels is related to how many people he feels deeply connected to—how many people are in his heart.

Men who wrestle with severe depression have a profound need for deep interpersonal connections. It's not that other men don't need or want these as well, but your band of brothers has a deep need for these connections. You experience horrific stress when your interpersonal needs are not met, whether that's because you've been shattered by losing someone you love or you've struggled to find people with whom you can truly connect in the first place. The pain you feel if you have been rejected is excruciating.

The Beast also knows about this deep need of yours. It knows that you hate being rejected and does everything it can to convince you that you can protect yourself from this pain by avoiding other people. It wants you to isolate yourself. It wants you to lock yourself in a jail cell. The more you isolate yourself, the lonelier you will be. The lonelier you are, the more depressed you will feel. The more depressed you feel, the more likely you are to engage in the self-defeating behaviors that feed the Beast.

The Prison of Social Isolation

When a man does not have enough deep social interactions, he becomes far more likely to experience severe depression. This is one of the reasons why solitary confinement is considered such a terrible punishment and is even used as a form of torture. People who are kept in solitary confinement for long periods of time often become mentally unhinged, psychotic, or even suicidal (Grassian 2006).

I want you to think about this fact: our brain evolved over millions of years, and we have direct evidence that for the last several hundred thousand years our ancestors lived in small groups, which involved constant social interaction (Hill,

Barton, and Hurtado 2009). Our ancestors woke up each day with other people, spent the day with other people, and went to sleep each night surrounded by other people. Of course, there must have been times when the proverbial lone hunter was off in the woods, silently stalking game, but his family, his group, his tribe, was never far away. The brain you are using to read this book evolved in an environment of continual social interaction (Lieberman 2013).

Yet in our modern societies we have increasingly moved away from direct social interaction. Our cities, towns, and suburbs make it possible for us to not directly interact with other people for days on end. Social media and the digital age have increased our isolation. Many of us have virtual friends, virtual relationships, and virtual lives. Yet this virtual exis-tence is a traumatic insult to our neuroanatomy when it takes the place of real live social connections. Our brains evolved over millions of years nurtured by rambunctious social interac-tion, and positive, meaningful social connections are the life force for our existence (Lieberman 2013).

The Beast knows that if it can get you to avoid others and cut yourself off from meaningful interper-sonal engagement, you will feel lonely, depressed, and mis-erable. If the Beast had its way, it would put you in a Super-max prison where you are forced into complete isolation

for twenty-three hours a day for years and years, with no meaningful social contact and nothing to do all day but to ruminate over your loss. At this very moment, this is exactly where the Beast is trying to put you.

Strategies to Strengthen Connections and Free Yourself from Your Prison

Because the Beast does not want you to become less depressed, it does not want you to feel like you really matter to anyone else. As it tries to get you to isolate yourself and avoid engaging in meaningful interactions, it wants you to avoid asking yourself this question: *What can I do at this moment to actively strengthen my connections to other people?* As your guide, I am not suggesting that you go out and become the life of the party. Nor should you try to become everyone's best friend. What I am suggesting is much simpler. I want you to draw a diagram of your current relationships and interpersonal connections.

This quick exercise will give you a visual representation of your current social world. You'll need a piece of paper and a pen. In the center of the paper make a small circle the size of a quarter. This circle represents you, so put your initials in it. Now draw more quarter-sized circles around that circle, starting a few inches away. These circles represent different people in your life, so add their initials to them. Put the people closest to you in the circles closest to yours, and more casual acquaintances or people you don't interact with often in the circles farther away. Now draw a line from each outer circle to yours in the middle. You have now created a visual diagram of the network of connections in which you exist.

But what if I don't have any damn connections? What if there is no one in my life who cares about me? If that's your reaction, you may be going about this exercise a bit wrong. The people in those outer circles are not necessarily people who *you* think care about you. They are just people in your life whom you know, including people at work, people in your neighborhood, family members, distant cousins, and, of course, new or old friends you have. The goal of this drawing is to simply make a visual representation of where you are at this moment.

As you practice the techniques I present in the rest of the book, my hope is that your network of interpersonal connections will become deeper and more complex. Just like the small, twisted strands of metal that make up powerful steel cables, the more real interpersonal connections you make, and add to your diagram, the stronger and more secure you will feel.

> **Do this to take energy away from the Beast:** Each morning send a brief email or text to a different person in your contact list. It could be a short "Hi, how are you?" or a link to something the individual may find interesting. Remind yourself that it doesn't matter if the person sends anything back. You are simply doing this to let the person know you are thinking about him or her. For every person on your contact list that you might like to see more of, try to reach out at least once every two months.

In the following sections I offer three strategies for building meaningful relationships and significantly strengthening interpersonal connections. Each strategy directly changes the neurochemistry in your brain. How? As you increase meaningful social connections and bond with other people, your brain releases more of the neurotransmitter oxytocin, which, in turn, stimulates the release of serotonin, which helps you feel much better (Lieberman 2007; Kiser et al. 2012). Positively changing the neurochemistry in your brain steals energy from the Beast. Here are the three strategies:

1. Listening for feelings (active listening)

2. Directly asking for what you would like (assertive speaking)

3. *Tikkun olam* ("Repairing the broken world")

Listening for Feelings (Active Listening)

The strongest way to connect to other people is to learn how to listen to them. When you actively listen for what another person is feeling, not only will you understand more about what the other person is experiencing, but you will simultaneously make him or her feel much more understood by you, that you "get it." *Listening for feelings is a direct way to change the neurochemistry in your brain,* too, because the more you feel connected to another person, the more oxytocin your brain produces (Lieberman 2007). This hormone not only makes you feel good, but it also prods your brain to produce more of the hormone serotonin, which will make you feel much less depressed (Kiser et al. 2012).

Active listening is one of the most powerful gifts you can give someone else. When someone feels you have really listened to them, they will feel understood by you. They will feel like you truly "get it" if they feel like you are paying attention to what they are emotionally going through. This is the process that underlies authentic connection. The more they feel you have listened to their emotional reactions, the deeper they feel the connection.

The secret to learning how to listen deeply is to focus on what the other person is feeling. As a psychologist, the primary tool of my trade is listening. The reason people raise their voices, from loud to yelling to screaming, is that they don't feel they are being heard, that their emotions aren't being heard. The reason people typically don't yell at a therapist, even when talking about scary or powerful things, is because they feel like the therapist is validating their emotional experience—that is, the therapist recognizes, acknowledges, and accepts their feelings. Thus, they feel deeply heard. The more that people feel like you are paying attention to their feelings, the more they will want to connect with you.

When I am listening to someone I care about, I am specifically trying to keep this question in mind: what are they feeling? I want to understand the emotional experience they are having and what it is like for them. But, as a man, this process can be very difficult for me. Why? Because like many men, when I was young I received very limited training in the arena of listening for feelings. I was taught to identify problems and offer solutions, not to identify emotions and validate feelings.

Approaching problems as puzzles that need to be fixed is a wonderful skill. In the workplace it is highly valued, and people can often earn a damn good living doing it. But when it comes to forming deeper connections with people we care about, this skill can be quite limiting. Many men fall into a trap by rushing in and offering advice. They will listen to the other person's problems for a few moments but then interrupt and offer a tidy solution. The difficulty you will have with this quick-fix "half-listening followed by giving helpful advice" approach is that no matter how clever your solution is, the other person will usually end up feeling like you haven't fully listened. When you jump in and offer up a solution to the problem without validating the feelings behind the problem, the person is going to think *He didn't hear a word I said.*

This is where active listening comes in. It's a five-step strategy for engaging others in a manner that leaves them feeling like you really did hear every word they said.

1. Start by biting down on your inner cheeks so you don't interrupt. That's right, *keep your mouth shut when the other person is talking!* This is key if you have the habit of breaking in when someone else is speaking. If you try this and find that you are still interrupting, you need to bite down harder. Bite until it hurts. Do not talk over others; do not cut in. Just let them speak.

2. Listen for the feeling and emotion. For example, if someone says, "I am really stressed at work," the emotion in question is *stress.* If someone complains about the traffic on the drive home, the emotion she's feeling is *frustration.*

3. Directly ask others what they are feeling. If you can't figure out what the other person is feeling, just come straight out and ask, "So, what are you feeling?" This step is one of the most effective tools for creating deep connection. The more you use this question, the better.

Do this to bleed energy from the Beast: Ask the other person, "So, what are you feeling?"

4. Repeat back to others the feeling they said they are having. This step is fairly simple, but a lot of guys screw it up, especially when talking to women. In this step you let others know that you truly heard them. A great way to do this is to begin with "Sounds like you are…" and then repeat the emotion they just told you they are having.

For example, after someone tells you about how difficult her day was, this would be the time to say "It sounds like you are really stressed at work." Or if she was talking about how long it took to drive home, it may help to say "That traffic sounds horrible. It's got to be frustrating."

It's essential that you don't invalidate what the person is feeling. That is, when a person describes a situation and says he felt a certain way, don't doubt it, argue against it, deny it, or try to fix it. For example, don't say "Really? You're not usually so thin-skinned," or "You shouldn't let your coworkers get to you," or "That's nothing. Let me tell you about my day," or "You should tell off that boss of yours." Rather, the goal is to actively validate the individual's reality. When it comes to feelings, there is no right or wrong; they are what they are. When you are trying to connect, your job is to let others know that you are trying to see things from their point of view.

When trying to validate someone else's experience, try to avoid the pitfall of one-upping the person. For example, if your friend is talking about what a rough day he had, telling him about how awful your day was will not help you to connect with him. When you do this, he will feel like you are competing with him, even belittling him. He will think you are not really interested in listening to what he is saying.

5. Do not offer a solution or clever advice. This may be the hardest step, because you are going to have to force yourself not to do something you may be dying to do, which is to offer advice. Right now you may be thinking, *What if there was a simple solution to the problem? If my wife had simply taken the shortcut I told her about, she could have missed all the crazy traffic. Then she wouldn't have gotten frustrated in the first place. Problem solved.* This might be true, but it doesn't matter if you are absolutely right about the shortcut. By offering your brilliant solution you've lost the chance to deepen your connection with the frustrated person. Remember, the goal with active listening is to connect with the feelings of someone you care about and want to have a better relationship with, not to solve or fix a problem.

Don't forget your solution, or clever advice; rather, save it for the very end of your talk, or even a quieter moment later on. Try something like this: "That drive sounds incredibly frustrating. It is lousy that you have to go through it every day. When I was listening to you, I suddenly remembered that there may be a way to avoid it, but I wasn't sure if it was the time to talk about that. I don't want to start giving advice, because I am sort of worried it is going to sound like a lecture, but if you do want to hear it later, please let me know." Do you see the nuance in this example? The guy is asking his wife if she's *interested* in hearing his advice instead of just jumping in and giving it.

Active listening takes practice. It can be especially hard to do with people you care about, because you want to protect them from negative experiences. You want to make things better for loved ones. I understand that urge. I want to support you in that goal, but the way to make them feel better, to protect them, is to first validate their emotional experience and make them feel truly heard by you.

What if you are listening to someone and don't like his emotional response? What if it sounds like BS? So what if you don't agree with it or you feel something different? This person is not having your response, because he's having his. Sometimes it is helpful to take a step back and remember this fact: this person is different from me and is having a different response. In the moment, when you are trying to connect with others through active listening, the emotional response they are having matters more than your interpretation of it.

Though active listening requires focused concentration, the good news is it doesn't require you to spend additional energy trying to come up with a solution to the other person's problems. Not having to solve the problems of people you care about is a wonderful thing. Once you realize that you no longer have to come up with clever solutions, you will feel much less reluctant to ask others what they are feeling. The more you ask people you care about what they are feeling, the more energy you will take away from the Beast.

In summary, to be a skilled active listener, do this:

1. Start by biting down on your inner cheeks so you don't interrupt.

2. Listen for the feeling and emotion.

3. If you don't know what someone is feeling, directly ask "So, what are you feeling?"

4. Repeat back to others the feeling they said they are having.

5. Do not offer a solution or clever advice.

ADVANCED LISTENING

When the speaker is done talking, instead of just repeating back to them the emotions they spoke about, ask them to elaborate on their emotional experience. For example, if they are talking about feeling stressed out and overwhelmed, say something like "Yes, I hear that you are feeling very stressed, and I can imagine this must be really hard, but can you tell me more about what the stress is like for you?"

This is the most powerful and, at the same time, most difficult thing to do when the person is describing a negative emotion, such as sadness or anger, that is directed at you and blaming you for causing it. For example, if your partner says "I am really pissed off at you because you never listen to me," a good advanced-listening reply might be "I hear that you are really angry at me. And, truthfully, I think I am getting a little defensive, because this is hard for me to hear. But can you tell me more about the anger? Seriously, I really want to hear more."

It may initially be problematic for the speaker. Depending on how angry the person is, he or she may not know how to respond. They may doubt your sincerity and wonder if you're playing with them. How can they trust that this is not just another ploy, or perhaps some type of psychobabble? If you can remain centered and trust the process (that is, believe in yourself, that you really do want to connect more deeply), you can ask again. "You said you were pissed off at me because it seems like I never listen. You are right; there are lots of times when I don't listen very well. But at this moment, I don't want to make the same mistake. I don't want you to walk away feeling like I didn't listen. I promise I will keep my mouth shut. Tell me more about your anger, please."

The secret to advanced listening is that it creates a paradox for the person who is talking. As soon as someone feels like you are really listening, like you really understand his or her anger, negative feelings toward you will begin to dissipate. The more the other person feels like you are listening and understanding their emotions, the less angry that person will be.

The essential feature to remember is that it is the act of listening that does the healing and furthers the connection you have to the other person. It's not the clever problem solving. So shut up! Don't fix, just listen. This wonderful quote, which has been attributed to different people, makes this point more elegantly: "People rarely remember what you say; what they almost always remember is how you made them feel" (Evans 1971, 244).

Here are the steps for advanced listening:

1. When a person you care about is expressing a negative feeling about you, such as "I am really angry at you," bite down even harder on your inner cheek so you don't interrupt.

2. When the person is done talking, tell him or her you are feeling a little anxious and a bit defensive, but you want to hear more about his or her anger, especially the angry feeling toward you.

3. While the person is talking, consciously try to slow down your breathing.

4. When the person is done talking, repeat back to him or her the feeling he or she is having toward you.

5. Try very hard not to explain or defend yourself, unless the person specifically asks for an explanation.

Directly Asking for What You Would Like (Assertive Speaking)

Assertive speaking is directly asking for what you really want. Asking another person for what you want takes energy away from the Beast because it will help you to feel much more in control of your life. The more you feel in control of your life, the less depression you will experience.

When it comes to getting what you want from other people, the Beast is going to do everything it can to convince you that you are helpless. The more helpless it can get you to believe you are, the more hopeless you will feel and the stronger your depression will become. In order to succeed in making you feel helpless, especially when you really want something from another person, the Beast has to figure out a way to make you feel terribly disempowered. It will do everything it can do to make you believe that you don't have the ability to get what you really want from someone else.

How does the Beast make you feel completely disempowered? It waits for the moment when you are feeling frustrated with someone, and then it uses the mind trick of overgeneralization to flood your mind with vague, large, and very important-sounding thoughts, such as *He doesn't* respect *me*, or *She doesn't* care about *me*, or *My friend doesn't* like *me*. When you come up with an overgeneralized thought, you rely upon one small bit of negative data regarding your current interaction with the other person and ignore any positive things that may have happened between the two of you. The Beast wants you to ruminate on these overgeneralized thoughts because it is trying to divert your attention. It is trying to get you more upset so you stop trying to figure out what it is you can do at this moment with your own behavior (including what you say) to get what you really want. The more you ruminate, the more disempowered you will feel, and the happier the Beast will be.

And here is the sly trick: the Beast knows that feeling *respected* and being *liked* and *cared about* are important to all of us. However, these words are problematic because they can't be clearly defined in a universal way. For example, if I tell my friend that I want her to respect me, the word "respect" itself is vague, and my friend may have a whole different understanding of what it means. How can that be? Isn't there just one standard definition you can find in any dictionary? The reality is that defining these "big idea" words is not about dictionaries. It is about families. Because we are all brought up in different families, we've had different experiences; thus, words like "respect," "care," and "like" mean different things to us. Even siblings who were brought up in the same family, lived in the same house, or played with the same pets will end up having different experiences, and these same words take on different meanings. The more the Beast gets you to use these vague words with the people you want something from, the less chance you have of actually getting it.

However, you can increase your sense of control in life, and take energy away from the Beast, using the technique of assertive speaking. These four steps will make you more effective at getting what you want.

1. Operationalize the thing you want by turning it into a set of very specific behaviors. When the Beast has you ruminating over big universal concepts, such as being respected, liked, or cared for, you can challenge it by pushing your mind to go as specific as possible. Start by asking yourself what specific behaviors make up these global, vague, big concepts. Called *operationalizing a concept*, this is the process of turning a concept into an identifiable action. For example, if you feel like your boss does not respect you, ask yourself, *What specific behaviors would my boss have to do to show that he or she respects me?* If nothing comes to mind, try working backward by asking yourself what specific behaviors of the other person indicate he or she doesn't respect you. For example, you might think *Well, when my boss comes into the office, he goes around to everyone's cubicle except mine and says hello.* Now you've operationalized the vague big concept of "respect" into a specific action. In other words, you know what you want, which is for your boss to say hello to you in the morning. Great! Now what do you do with this? How do you get what you want? This brings us to step 2.

2. Other people are pretty much going to do what they want to do, so tell your mind it is wasting its energy when it obsesses over another person's behavior. The moment you identify what you want is the moment your Beast will use its second line of attack to try and make you feel disempowered: it will do everything it can to get you to focus your energy on the wrong person. Your Beast will try to convince you that what you need to do is change the other person's behavior. It does not want you to try and figure out how you can specifically change some aspect of your own behavior, including what you do and what you say.

I know this idea that you are supposed to focus on changing some aspect of your own behavior and not that of the other person may seem counterintuitive. Your gut is probably telling you that the problem is not you, it's the other person, because that is precisely what the Beast wants you to think. It wants you to think this because it wants you to feel helpless. It knows the more it gets you to focus your energy on changing the other person, the less chance you have of getting what you want. The Beast knows a basic rule of human behavior that I call "psychology rule #1": we have very little power to change other people's behavior because they are going to do pretty much what they want to do. I believe this is true of me and of you. I realize this sounds fairly hopeless in the context of getting what you want, and that is exactly how the Beast wants you to hear it. The Beast, however, will never tell you about the most important rule in psychotherapy, which I call the "prime directive."

3. Remember this prime directive, the most important rule of psychotherapy: we do have the power to change some of our own behavior, including what we say, and that means we are not helpless. When it comes to finding a more effective way to get what you want from other people, instead of focusing on the other person, the key is to figure out a way to change a small aspect of your own behavior. It is your behavior that changes the neurochemistry in your own brain. What you do in most situations has much greater impact on how depressed you will feel, regardless of whether or not the other person gives you what you want.

Again, this may sound counterintuitive. Most of us have been socialized to think that if people just respected us more, or were simply nicer to us, we would feel a lot better. When it comes to feeling horribly depressed, however, what actually changes depression, what actually bleeds energy away from the Beast, is not how you judge other people but how you judge yourself. Generally you will feel much less helpless, and much less depressed, if you judge yourself as a man who clearly and directly identifies what you would like and specifically asks for it.

4. Directly ask the other person for what you especially *would* like. The key here is to turn the specific behavior you want of the other person into a direct request by using the conditional word "would." Using this word turns your desire into a question, not a demand. People resent being told what to do. If they feel forced to do something, there is a good chance they will be pissed off at you, and even if they do what you want, their anger is going to come out in some way. If they don't do what you want, then you are going to feel angrier, and more helpless, which leads to greater feelings of depression. Structuring your desire as a request may make other people understand that you are giving them a choice. If they choose not to comply, then you can clearly see that they made a choice and not blame yourself.

And here's is the most important point to keep in mind with step 4, especially in terms of taking energy away from the Beast. Regardless of outcome, in the end we actually spend most of our energy judging ourselves for what we do or don't do, and not the actions of others. That is, if I see myself as someone who puts myself out there and directly asks for what I want, I will feel differently about myself than if I viewed myself as someone who never asks for what I want. In terms of one's self-concept and feeling depressed, it matters much more how we view ourselves than whether we always get what we want.

To see how this plays out, let's return to the example of the man who feels disrespected because his boss doesn't come over to his cubicle to say good morning. Instead of focusing on what the boss is doing, he could change some small aspect of his own behavior so that he has a better chance of getting what he wants. I'm not suggesting that he work harder, or show up at work earlier. I am talking about behavior change that is much more direct: the man could speak to his boss and ask for what he specifically would like. For example, "I do appreciate it when you touch base with me in the morning. I know you are busy, but it does help me make sure we are on the same page each day, and that I am doing what you want. Would it be possible to make this a routine thing?"

Directly asking for what you would like is both simple and difficult. It can be simple if you use a clear "I" statement and ask for a specific thing, but the Beast can make it difficult for you because its goal is still the same. It wants you to feel disempowered, and if it can't confuse you by getting you to obsess over the other person's behavior, and if getting you to use vague, huge global concepts didn't work, it will use its third line of attack: grabbing hold of your vocal cords. That is, it will either try to convince you to keep quiet and not say anything at all or raise your voice and yell. There isn't anything wrong with being quiet, and there are times when raising your voice is appropriate. When it comes to making a specific request of someone else, however, keeping your mouth shut doesn't work because no one can read your mind. Raising your voice doesn't work either. Whether you intend to or not, the other person will think you are yelling, and raising your voice always turns a request into a demand, and the other person will end up resenting you. The most effective delivery method is to directly and clearly ask the other person for something that you specifically would like. And remember, because you are using the phrase "I *would* like it if you...," you have turned the sentence into a request, and, as with any request, the other person has the right to say no.

Wait a second! After all this you are telling me I still may not get what I want? Yes, that's correct. When you make a request, other people can always say no. But it doesn't really matter what their answer is, because by making the request you are actually going to get what you want most, which is to stop feeling so damn depressed. The more often you directly ask others for what you specifically would like, the more you will view yourself as an effective and active man who directly engages the world and the people around you. You will experience yourself as less helpless, less disempowered, and less afraid to go after the things you want most. Even if you don't get what you asked for, you will feel better about yourself. This is one of those rare win-wins, because you benefit no matter what other people do. Their behavior is not as important as your own behavior. Regardless of whether or not the other person says yes or no, the very act of directly asking for what you would like will drain energy away from your Beast, and you will end up feeling better about yourself as a result.

In summary, when you want something from someone else, use the technique of assertive speaking:

1. Operationalize the thing you want by turning it into a set of very specific behaviors. The more specific actions you can identify the better. For example, it is not effective to tell someone they need an "attitude adjustment" because everyone defines that big concept differently. But it can be, "Would you put the plates in the dishwasher on Tuesday night?"

2. Other people are pretty much going to do what they want to do, so tell your mind it is wasting its energy when it obsesses over another person's behavior.

3. Remember this prime directive, the most important rule of psychotherapy: we do have the power to change some of our own behavior, including what we say, and that means we are not helpless.

4. Directly ask the other person for what you *would* like. Remind yourself that because you are making a request, not a demand, the other person has the right to say no.

While practicing assertive speaking, keep these three points in mind:

1. Try not to let the Beast grab your vocal cords and strangle your mouth shut. People cannot read your mind, and the Beast will feed off your passivity. On the other hand, don't let the Beast make your voice come out too loud. People will resent you if they feel like you are yelling at them, so try hard to speak directly and clearly without raising your voice.

2. If you are worried about being selfish by asking for what you want, remind yourself that it is a lot more selfish to expect other people to be able to read your mind.

3. Practice, practice, practice. The more you practice asking for what you specifically would like, the better you will get at it and the better you will feel. If you don't have a lot of experience asking for what you want, start by asking for something that is seemingly small, perhaps even trivial. For example, if you are eating at a table and you want hot sauce, ask for it. "Would you pass the hot sauce, please?" Practicing direct, small requests like that will make you feel more confident when asking for the bigger things you also want.

Tikkun Olam (Repairing the World)

Attached to a red steel girder in the middle of the Golden Gate Bridge is a sign that says, "The consequences of jumping from this bridge are fatal and tragic." That blue sign is part of a suicide-prevention effort to help those who feel desperate.

While writing this book I imagined what it would be like if under that sign, attached to the cold steel girder, there was a clear Plexiglas box filled with copies of this book, available to anyone who found themselves lost and in pain. Perhaps they would see the title and think it was a bit silly, but for a moment they might stop and open it and come to this exact page and read these words: The Beast of severe depression is a liar. The Beast has tricked you into doing a series of behaviors that have made you feel much more depressed. It is now telling you that all is hopeless, and the only way you can stop the pain is to end your life.

You can prove to yourself that the Beast is a liar, and that the only thing it wants is for you to feel more depressed. Has the Beast ever asked how you can add more meaning to your life? No, I didn't think so. The Beast knows there are ways that you can, but it doesn't want you to try.

While I love that question and endlessly find myself thinking about it, I don't know the answer that is right for you. The phrase *tikkun olam*, from Judaism, resonates with me. It means "repair the world" and is based on the premise that the world is broken, and yet we have the power to bring enormous meaning into our lives if we choose to try to make it a little better. This phrase can bring greater meaning to your life by deepening your connections to the people around you who need your strength.

Meaning can be found in trying to make things a little better. I find this to be an extraordinary idea. I'm not trying to convert you to Judaism, nor do I believe that this concept is unique to Judaism. I am writing about tikkun olam because I believe there is something here worth thinking about, especially as you are feeling dead to the world. Whether you are walking back and forth in that cold air on the Golden Gate Bridge or you are sitting in front of an electronic screen in a lonely bar, the question remains: How can you add more meaning to your life?

As noted earlier, severe depression is a behavioral, emotional, and physical syndrome that engulfs a person. One of its hallmarks is that it seeks to convince a person that his or her life has no meaning. Or, to make it more personal, the Beast has desperately sought to convince you that *your* life has no meaning. It emphatically wants you to experience a profound sense of disconnection from other people so you feel increasingly helpless, alienated, and alone.

But here is the problem with this thinking. While the Beast of severe depression seeks to isolate and disconnect you from others, the world itself is fragmented and very much needs your strength. Actually, what it needs *most* is your strength. Our fragmented world needs you to personally and directly engage with it. This is an acute paradox, isn't it? Here you are feeling your very worst—some of you may even be thinking of throwing yourself off a bridge—and I am clearly saying the world needs you. *But what can one person do?* you may wonder. *How can any one person make a difference?*

It does not matter what horrifying statistic one focuses on. Whether it's the seventeen thousand children across the world who are going to die today because they did not get enough to eat (World Hunger 2015), or the unknown number of people who are dying of loneliness because no one has spoken to them for days on end, the pain of the world is excruciating. The world is broken: global warming, rising sea levels, environmental trauma, mass extinctions—and this is just a small list of the world's problems.

What can one man do? What can you do? While I don't know what answer is right for you, I do know three things that might help you answer them for yourself. The first is that the Beast is a liar. There are things that need to be done today, wherever you live, and you have the power to do them. The second is that *Other people are hurting, and I am going to try to help some of them* is a powerful and courageous thought that is the opposite of despair. And the third is that if you consciously make a decision to act—regardless of how small or seemingly insignificant the act appears—it alone will do more to steal energy from the Beast than anything else I have suggested. And regardless of whether or not the world changes or even notices, *you* will change. You will experience meaning, and you will stop feeling so damn depressed.

However, the benefits don't stop there. If you make a choice to act, to move toward the world, you will no longer be alone. By making the private decision to commit a small act to improve your community, you move out of your private, isolated hell and place yourself within a group of other men who have also made the exact same decision. These men have also had the courageous thought *People are hurting, and I am going to try and help some of them.*

This group, of course, is not limited to men. Most of the folks in this group have never met each other, yet if you decide to move toward the world, to take one small action to try to help, you make yourself a vital member. The others may not know your name, but you become one of them.

I know this probably sounds strange, but the decision to act upon this world, to try in your own small way to make it a little better, aligns you with others who are also trying to make this broken world a little better. This struggle can imbue your life with extraordinary meaning. This is absolutely true! It is the opposite of despair. As you commit to further acts of repair, of action without expectation, you will feel increasingly empowered. The Beast will lose more energy, and you will feel significantly less depressed.

Protect Yourself by Protecting Your Community

The word "protect" has been co-opted by gun culture. It has become a code word for carrying a gun, or a lens through which to view strangers as potential enemies. If you walk around anxiously scanning everyone as a potential threat, that continual worry will feed your Beast. Therefore, I want to offer you a different way to think about the word "protect." If you do something to help someone on your street, in your town, or in your city, you are helping to protect your community. Psychologists call this prosocial behavior, and research has shown that it increases the production of serotonin, which helps you feel better. It not only helps others but protects you from your Beast (Raposa, Laws, and Ansell 2016).

Years ago I worked with a man who wrestled with horrible depression that surfaced as intense feelings of irritability and terrible road rage. His commute took about thirty minutes, but no matter how many anger-management strategies he tried, such as consciously slowing down his breathing and reminding himself that the only thing that mattered was getting to work safely, nothing worked. He would pull into the office parking lot with a red face and high blood pressure, stewing about all the lousy drivers on the road. His day was ruined just as it was getting started.

This went on for years, until one frigid winter morning he saw a car lose control and spin into a ditch. He immediately pulled over and helped the person get out. The young driver was pretty shaken up but not hurt, and after calling the state highway patrol he gave her a lift to a convenience store down the road. As he drove away from the store, he suddenly thought, *My job is to offer drivers help.* With that simple thought he turned himself into a one-man volunteer AAA roadside service. He bought a pair of jumper cables, which he put into his trunk, along with a flashlight, umbrella, blanket, and water bottles. On his way to work he would scan the road for cars on the shoulder and offer help to anyone who seemed like they could use a hand. I asked him how often he actually used the cables, and he said almost never, but that didn't matter. What mattered was that his road rage disappeared. He now saw himself as helping to protect his community, and he went from seeing other drivers as aggressive strangers to neighbors whom he had not met. He could recognize that they were also just trying to get to work.

His actions didn't end with the simple thought *My job is to offer drivers help*, nor with outfitting his car with useful items. He started volunteering for the American Red Cross and would travel throughout the state to wherever a new emergency shelter was opened. When others became worried because of hurricanes, he became energized because he now had a job to do, a place where he was needed. He told me that this direct engagement in his community drained the energy out of the Beast.

If a man doesn't feel that he is deeply needed, he may ask himself, *Why live?* I can't speak for your partner, or for your family, but I do know that your community needs you. There are specific people who are living in your community who are hurting at this moment, and they need your strength. They need *you*. Not someone else—not a social worker, not a nurse, not a million dollars. What they need is you. How do I know this? Because the most terrible disease out there is loneliness. Nothing is more devastating. Nothing is more destructive. It is the haunting specter of our time. In the end it is loneliness that breaks us. But you are not without power. You have the ability to change your own neurochemistry by transforming the life of a complete stranger. To do this you just have to remember that you are choosing to give and not asking for or expecting anything in return.

I know the Beast tells you that you can protect yourself by keeping away from other people. *Watch out! Don't get too close! People will always let you down in the end. And no one really cares*

about you anyway. Your severe depression is doing everything it can to deepen your feeling of helplessness, because it is terrified that you will eventually figure out the one thought that can kill it: *I have the power to positively transform the lives of other people.*

I met another guy who engaged with his community by getting involved with Habitat for Humanity. It happened during a bad recession when he was an unemployed IT guy. His depression had him locked in his apartment. His days were spent lying on the couch playing video games, punctuated by bouts of fruitlessly applying for jobs. This cycle kept him spiraling downward until he read that Habitat for Humanity was building a house in his town. He knew about the organization, but he hesitated contacting anyone involved because he was not part of a church and was embarrassed that he didn't know a damn thing about carpentry. Then he read on their website that all volunteers were welcome. If you just showed up, other volunteers would teach you what to do. He went for four hours twice a week and learned basic carpentry, including how to operate a circular saw, frame a room, and hang drywall. Eventually he did get another IT position, but he kept working with Habitat for Humanity on Saturday mornings because, he told me, he was now part of the crew, and they needed him. Most of all he said it helped him feel better.

While both the American Red Cross and Habitat for Humanity are great organizations, there are many severely depressed men, possibly including you, who are reading this who don't have the desire to get involved with a community volunteer organization. So I want to offer you another simple, and somewhat dramatic, guerrilla technique to attack that fog of helplessness. You can do it on your own, but it still helps protect the community you live in. Get a large plastic trash bag and go pick up the garbage along the side of a road until you fill it. Then throw it into a dumpster. By doing this small but dramatic act, you attacked your Beast head-on because you have suddenly exerted control over your life. No one has demanded that you do this unusual thing, voluntarily picking up other people's garbage, but making a conscious choice to do this prosocial behavior will have helped your community. Even more importantly, this very action, where you are trying to help other people, will change how you feel because it will begin to increase the amount of dopamine and oxytocin in your brain (Raposa et al. 2016).

No, picking up trash will not instantly cure your depression, but it will absolutely take away some of the Beast's energy. It is a fantastic gesture that clearly tells the Beast you are sick and tired of feeling helpless. You are refusing to submit to nothingness. You are seizing control of your own life.

The Beast will not be pleased and will try to stop you by raising your anxiety and warning you that you will end up making a fool of yourself by picking up garbage along the road. If you hear inner thoughts like this, you are on the right track. However, if the fear of potential public humiliation (that is, you're afraid of being seen by someone you know) feels overwhelming, start by picking up garbage along a stream off in the woods. Or, choose a remote part of a city park. You can find crap—plastic bags half submerged in mud, tires lining the floor of a creek bed—to pick up everywhere. You might even be able to recycle some of the items you find. You can start your own environmental revolution.

If you are thinking this the stupidest suggestion you have ever heard, that's exactly the point. This technique works precisely because it is unusual. To help repair your severe depression—which again can be thought of as a gash in your brain—you need to take *drastic measures*.

Furthermore, to make this guerrilla technique even more powerful, try to tell as few people as possible about what you are up to, preferably no one. That's right; ideally you will get your butt out the door, clean up trash that isn't your responsibility, not get paid for it, and then not tell anyone you did it. Sounds crazy, doesn't it? Yes, that is why it works. Action without expectation. You are not doing this for anyone else— you are doing it for yourself.

Chapter 4

Depression and Psychotherapy

I want to admit two things to you. First, I love that you are reading my book. It is really a great feeling to know that someone is reading the words I wrote and that they may be helpful. Second—and this is much more important—*this book is not nearly enough*. What I mean is that self-help books such as this one are best at outlining a series of techniques a person can utilize on his own. And books like this are often a decent first step for many people. But when you are talking about the gale-force winds involved in the cyclone of depression, a man needs more than just helpful techniques. He needs to engage in a deep, ongoing, life-affirming relationship with another human being through psychotherapy. He needs to be engaged in *psychotherapy*, which can go much, much deeper than this book—provided there is a good fit between client and therapist. Sitting down in a quiet room with a therapist and talking about what is in your heart deeply transforms the neurochemistry in your brain (Karlsson 2011). In this chapter, I'll discuss what to expect in therapy, what to look for in a therapist, my recommendations for treating your depression, and what to consider when weighing the benefits of antidepressants.

Recommendations for Treating Severe Depression

If I had a magic wand and could place you in the best treatment for depression available, the following is what I would recommend.

Individual psychotherapy with an experienced psychotherapist. First, I would want to see you get into a powerful psychotherapeutic relationship with a therapist. This needs to be a good match, one in which you feel like the therapist is trying hard to really listen to you and get to know you as a person. Your gut will tell you if the therapist is the right fit: someone you can trust and open your heart to.

A consultation with a psychiatrist regarding medication. In addition to engaging in ongoing individual psychotherapy, I would want you to consult with a psychiatrist about whether adding medication to your treatment may be helpful. The psychiatrist you work with should collaborate closely with your psychotherapist, and he or she should also seek to connect with you as an individual who has a unique life story, and not just as a patient with a diagnosis.

An interpersonal psychotherapy process group. Besides ongoing, long-term individual psychotherapy, I'd also like to see you participate in group therapy. Group psychotherapy is a powerful venue for healing. It can be particularly helpful to anyone wrestling with severe depression. I would recommend joining a therapy group that utilizes a relational/process group format. An interpersonal psychotherapy process group is composed of the same small group of people who get together each week to talk with one another about what is happening (or not happening) in their lives, including what is going on in their relationships, families, and jobs. Most important, people in these groups discuss what they are really feeling deep inside. The authentic encounter among the people in the room as they get to know each other over time creates a space for profound healing. And, yes, I would strongly recommend that you join a slow jogging group, or, better yet, create your own! But you may have to build on these other stages first.

Antidepressant Medications

Severe depression is an absolutely horrible behavioral, emotional, and physical syndrome that affects every part of a man's being. Left untreated it will end in death for tens of thousands of men (AAS 2014). This figure relates to death through suicide, but it is much higher when the effects of alcohol and other substances, as well as numerous car "accidents," are considered. For these reasons, it's important to consider whether or not antidepressant medications might benefit you.

It is also important to note that while we invented the words "biology" and "psychology," to the brain they are the same thing. We have created these categories as a way to help us understand what is happening in the brain and in the mind, but these divisions are artificial and constantly undergoing revision. It is not a simple question of whether your depression is caused just by problems with your brain chemicals (aka biology), or if it is "all in your head" (aka psychology). The biology of the brain and the psychology of the mind are constantly interacting and continually changing each other. Remember this point if your Beast is whispering in your ear that all you need to do is just take a pill and you will be fine.

Another thing to bear in mind when considering whether meds might be right for you is that most pharmaceutical advertising is BS. Like all marketing for multibillion-dollar corporations, it accentuates the positive and minimizes the negative. *There are no happy pills.* Regardless of whether or not you take an antidepressant medication, you will still have to confront many of the same problems. The pills do not make them go away, nor do the pills teach you anything—particularly more effective ways to cope with the problems you are facing. This is what psychotherapy is for.

Antidepressant medications do seem to be able to positively target some of the physical (somatic) symptoms of severe depression, including helping a person feel less exhausted, and easing body aches and pains. Many men report that the heavy weight on their shoulders becomes lighter, or that they no longer feel like they are trudging through three feet of molasses. The medications may not put a smile on their face, but they do report feeling less awful, and that that feeling has certainly been worth any inconveniences or side effects related to the medications.

Many clients have reported that another common positive effect of taking medications is that their anxiety seems less pressing. Before the medication, many felt consumed by horrifying worry, but as the meds kicked in they began to experience anxiety as something separate from them, that they had a bit of distance from their worries. The anxiety didn't disappear, but they had some breathing room. They said this bit of distance from their own anxiety gave them room to operate and figure out what to do, instead of just being consumed by it.

When I talk to a client who is considering taking antidepressants, I offer several recommendations and suggestions. First, find a provider who has a lot of experience treating severe depression. Typically this would be a psychiatrist, but other medical providers who have trained in the field of mental health may also be very good. What I don't want to see happen, however, is for a severely depressed man to get a prescription for an inadequate dose of an antidepressant from a provider who is poorly trained to treat severe depression or, even worse, not committed to seeing the patient for ongoing care. Severe depression is a serious chronic disease, and ongoing follow-up care is essential. Patients need to be repeatedly monitored to see how the antidepressant medications are affecting them, and dosages often need to be adjusted for maximum benefit.

Second, I encourage you to approach taking medication from a scientific point of view. I believe it is crucial to conceive of taking an antidepressant medication as though you have set up an experiment in which you are the one subject in the study. As the single subject, it is very important to consistently record data on the pluses and minuses of taking the medication. Every medication affects every system in the body, which is not a problem in and of itself. However, in this study you are trying to determine whether the positive effects outweigh potential negative side effects, so it's important to set up a log and keep a small record of all the changes, including both positive changes as well as any negative changes, in your mind and body.

Third, talk with your provider about the quality of your sleep. Though some sleep medications appear to cause more problems than they solve over the long term, some medications do help some people to sleep better over the short term. I encourage you to engage your doctor in a conversation about what medications he or she thinks may be helpful, and why. Remember, getting good sleep is a key to feeling better.

And lastly, it is important to bear in mind that antidepressant medications do not work instantly. It might be helpful to think of an antidepressant the way you think of fertilizer. When you fertilize a garden, you don't see instantaneous results, but four to six weeks later you should see an improvement. The same is true of antidepressants. However, if the antidepressant medication does not seem to be helping, it is really important not to throw in the towel. The science of psychiatry cannot yet determine which antidepressant medication will work best for each individual, but ongoing research in genetics and medication is trying to help answer that question. The science of psychiatry has shown—very convincingly so—that if you take your medication as prescribed and you keep seeing your provider, even if they have to try different antidepressants, there is a good chance you will find one that works well for you (NIMH 2008).

The point is, don't listen to your Beast when it whispers in your ear that there is nothing anyone can do. Stick with the treatment plan you and your provider arrive at, and you will prevail.

What Happens in Therapy?

Psychotherapy is both art and science, and each therapist utilizes a style that works best for him or her. As for my own style, here are some of the things I typically do, as well as some of the laws and codes of ethics I must abide by.

When someone sees me for therapy, the first thing I talk about is confidentiality. I go into depth about the rules of confidentiality, because I know there are some severely depressed men who will not contact a therapist because they are worried the therapist will not keep their information private. They worry that if they tell a therapist about all the thoughts running through their head, the therapist will think they are crazy and commit them to a psych ward, or the therapist will tell their wife, partner, family, or boss about what is going on. I understand these anxious thoughts, but the privacy that exists between me and a client is extremely important and legally protected by doctor–client privilege, which means that anything we discuss stays in the room. This is true for all licensed therapists.

It is my legal and ethical responsibility to protect a person's privacy, and I take this very seriously. If a client's wife, girlfriend, mother, or boss calls me, my response is like what you'd expect from the CIA, in that I neither confirm nor deny I have any idea who this person is talking about. I am willing to talk to another person about a client only if the client has given written consent to do so. And, under those circumstances, I tell my client everything I talked about with the other person.

While the privileged communication between therapist and client is protected by law, the law also mandates that I break confidentiality in several circumstances. The first is if a client tells me he is planning to kill himself in the immediate future. If someone tells me he is planning on committing suicide, I will break confidentiality and do my best to get him hospitalized. It is very important to note that disclosing *an imminent suicidal plan with intention to act* is very different from hearing a client say that he thinks about death a lot, has suicidal thoughts, or doesn't care if he wakes up tomorrow. As I noted earlier, suicidal ideation and thoughts of death are very common symptoms of severe depression. If a client tells me he's having these thoughts, I try to determine if he has access to guns or lethal pills, and how safe he feels with himself at this time.

If the client feels safe and does not intend to act on his thoughts about suicide and death, then they become part of our work together. It is very important to understand that telling a therapist you have been thinking about suicide and telling a therapist you are planning on killing yourself are two very different things. I don't want you to erroneously believe that if you say the word "suicide" to a therapist you are going to get locked up. That's simply not true.

Additionally, if a client tells me about current domestic violence or abuse of a child, a disabled person, or an elderly person, I will break confidentiality. In each of these cases I am required to immediately contact the appropriate government agencies. I am also legally required to break confidentiality if a client tells me he is planning on harming someone. Again, this is very different from a client discussing how angry he is at another person. I would view "Let me tell you what I'd like to do to that SOB..." as venting angry feelings. But if a client discloses that he has specific plans to hurt or kill a specific individual, then the law states that I must contact the police and try to warn that person.

Once I have gone over the rules of confidentiality, I pursue two goals. First, I find out as much about the client as I can, and second, I try to connect with him as best I can. While I am very interested in understanding why he is coming to see me and what his symptoms are, I generally start with questions regarding the client's history: Where did you grow up? Do you have siblings? Are your folks still together? Then I try to find out if the client is in a relationship and, if so, what that is like. I am also very interested in what his inner circle looks like— that is, who does he really care about and who does he feel supported by? Gathering the details of someone's life helps me to best understand his symptoms.

When choosing a new therapist, I always tell clients to listen to their gut. I suggest that after meeting with me a few times, they should ask themselves, *Does this feel like someone I can eventually open up to and perhaps one day learn to trust?* If their gut says yes, then they are on the right track.

If something doesn't feel right, the best thing to do is to tell the therapist this during the next session. Therapists spend years and years training, so they should be able to handle this directness. Most therapists are pleased when new clients tell them what they are feeling. If the therapist you're working with is not a good match for you, he or she may be able to help you find a better fit. If it is a good match, remind yourself that the therapy process takes time. Your problems did not start yesterday, and you are not going to get them to go away by tomorrow. As your guide I strongly encourage you to commit to sticking with therapy. The more you invest in yourself, the more likely you are to permanently transform your life.

Therapy is a place to talk about your feelings. I wouldn't be surprised if your Beast just read that and is whispering in your ear, *Real men don't talk about feelings. Can you imagine John Wayne in therapy?* Actually, this quote, from the actor Marion Morrison (aka John Wayne), is a curious one to ponder when thinking about what it means to be a man. "When I started, I knew I was no actor and I went to work on this Wayne thing… It was as deliberate a projection as you'll ever see. I figured I needed a gimmick, so I dreamed up the drawl, the squint and a way of moving meant to suggest that I wasn't looking for trouble but would just as soon throw a bottle at your head as not. I practiced in front of a mirror" (Shepard 1979). By many accounts, John Wayne is the archetypal American manly man, yet "John Wayne" was just a persona, a role Morrison played. He wasn't real.

In my experience, the strong silent types are often the lonely depressed types. And it wouldn't surprise me if many depressed men avoid therapy because they believe that talking about their pain will mean they are weak. I strongly believe that talking about what you are truly experiencing will make you stronger as a man. In addition, talking about your true feelings with someone who really listens, and who really cares, changes your brain chemistry (Karlsson 2011). It directly drains energy from the Beast and helps you to feel better.

Conclusion

Do Something to Starve the Beast Every Day

The number one thought I want you to take away from this book is this: *Every day I will do some specific thing to take energy away from my depression.* This is probably the most important thing I try to get my depressed clients to think about. The issue is not what you are going to do next year, or next month, or even tomorrow, it is what are you going to do today. What are you going to do *now*?

Each day when you get up in the morning, ask yourself this question. I strongly encourage you to write it down and tape it to your bathroom mirror: *What specific thing am I going to do today to steal energy from my depression?* No matter how lousy you are feeling, keep asking yourself this question. *What specific thing am I going to do today to steal energy away from my depression?* The smaller and more direct the action is, the more effective it will be. Your Beast will want you to come up with some enormous plan, such as an overwhelming New Year's resolution (for example, "This year I will be a better person." Or "I am really going to get in shape."). It wants you to think about these impossible resolutions because it knows they are too broad, and after you stop trying to do them you will feel even more depressed. Fight your Beast by focusing on this very moment. When your mind goes big and vague, force it to go small and specific. Don't forget: *the smaller and more direct the action, the more powerful it will be.*

What if you are feeling so damn depressed that you simply can't do anything because you don't have the energy? If that's the case, go back and take a look at the pictures in this book. Start at the beginning, look at each illustration, and think about whether it has any relevance for you. Then get ahold of a piece of paper and capture the Beast with words. That is, write down exactly how you are feeling at this very moment. An example might be something like *I am feeling like crap right now. I really don't want to do this. Utter BS. Damn! I am absolutely miserable, totally exhausted. Even thinking about this makes me tired.*

Every sentence you write steals energy from the Beast. You may not feel better instantly, but this process does work. It's like taking a blowtorch to an iceberg. Do it long enough, and you will eventually see progress. If you happen to be one of those lucky people who can draw or paint, then try illustrating how you feel. The movement of your hand will deny the Beast what it wants most: for you to be still. The goal is to do precisely what the Beast does not want you to do, which is to act, to create, and to break your silence.

Now that you are at the end of this book, I want to remind you of this strange but true concept: your Beast is also at the end of this book. It sat on your shoulder while you held this book and also has read every word and every sentence that you have read. At this very moment the Beast is probably whisper-ing in your ear, *I told you that this self-help garbage was all crap. This guy knows nothing of the things you're dealing with; he hasn't a clue about your problems—problems he could never dream of. Your problems can never be solved... Maybe this stuff might help someone else, but there's no way it's going to help you.* This is the cynical voice of the Beast. It desperately wants you to feel as helpless as possible, to live without hope. It wants you to do nothing, to live in despair. It wants you to disappear. Remember, your Beast is a liar.

Though we have not met, I do know this about you: you are stronger and more courageous than your Beast. I know this is true because there is a part of you that wants to feel better. That is why you read this book. That part of you is stronger than your Beast. It is an absolute fact. At this very moment you have the strength to change the neurochemicals that underlie the horrible depression in your brain, by changing small aspects of your behavior. Use the part of you that wants to feel better to push back at the helpless, cynical voice of your Beast. Identify one small action. Take one single step. This is the essence of courage. No one can take this away from you, not the people around you, not your genes, and not your Beast. Underneath the fog of all of your current problems, and your unbearable pain, lies a deep lake of resiliency. You have coped with many difficult times in your past, and you have made it here to this exact moment. Draw strength from your reservoir now. Read this book again and again. Take that crucial first step against your Beast and you will begin to stop feeling so damn depressed.

Acknowledgments

This book exists because of the unending support of my wife, Amy. She is the embodiment of graceful strength, perseverance, and kindness. Her love endlessly stuns me. I would also like to thank my friends and family whose names make up my heart. Your unflinching support is deeply felt. I am particularly grateful to Ralph Hardy, Richard Goldberg, and Stephen Ingram, whose thoughtful comments helped this book move forward. In addition, I would like to thank Caleb Beckwith, who provided farsighted editorial feedback that helped bridge the chasm between my thoughts and my words.

Resources

Recommended Books:

Burns, D. D. 1980. *Feeling Good: The New Mood Therapy*. New York: HarperCollins.

Burns, D. D. 1990. *The Feeling Good Handbook*. New York: Plume.

McGonigal, K. 2015. *The Upside of Stress: Why Stress Is Good for You, and How to Get Good at It*. New York: Avery.

Real, T. 1997. *I Don't Want to Talk About It: Overcoming the Secret Legacy of Male Depression*. New York: Scribner.

Recommended Websites

Alcoholics Anonymous, http://www.aa.org

Narcotics Anonymous, https://www.na.org

National Suicide Prevention Lifeline (1-800-273-8255), http://www.suicidepreventionlifeline.org

https://www.youtube.com (Search for "human kindness" and watch the videos that come up.)

References

AACC (American Association for Clinical Chemistry). 2015. "Any Dose of Alcohol Combined with Cannabis Significantly Increases Levels of THC in Blood." *ScienceDaily.* May 27, 2015. www.sciencedaily.com/releases/2015/05/150527112728.htm.

AAS (American Association of Suicidology). 2014. "Depression and Suicide Risk." https://www.suicidology.org/portals/14/docs/resources/factsheets/2011/depressionsuicide2014.pdf.

APA (American Psychiatric Association). 2000. *Diagnostic and Statistical Manual of Mental Disorders.* 4th ed. Rev. Washington, DC: APA.

Attenborough, W. 2014. *Churchill and the 'Black Dog' of Depression: Reassessing the Biographical Evidence of Psychological Disorder.* Palgrave Macmillan.

Avena, N. M., P. Rada, and B. G. Hoebel. 2008. "Evidence for Sugar Addiction: Behavioral and Neurochemical Effects of Intermittent, Excessive Sugar Intake." *Neuroscience and Biobehavioral Reviews* 32 (1): 20–39.

Awopetu, A.R. 2014. "A Review of the Physiological Effects of Exercise Duration and Intensity During Walking and

Jogging. *Journal of Emerging Trends in Educational Research and Policy Studies* 5 (6): 660–667.

Banerjee, N. 2014. "Neurotransmitters in Alcoholism: A Review of Neurobiological and Genetic Studies." *Indian Journal of Human Genetics* 20 (1): 20–31.

Blumenthal, J. A., P. J. Smith, and B. M. Hoffman. 2012. "Is Exercise a Viable Treatment for Depression?" *ACSM's Health and Fitness Journal* 16 (4): 14–21.

Boden, J. M., and D. M. Fergusson. 2011. "Alcohol and Depression." *Addiction* 106 (5): 906–914.

Booth, F. W., M. V. Chakravarthy, and E. E. Spangenburg. 2002. "Exercise and Gene Expression: Physiological Regulation of the Human Genome Through Physical Activity." *Journal of Physiology* 543 (pt. 2): 399–411.

Brooks, P. J. 1997. "DNA Damage, DNA Repair, and Alcohol Toxicity—A Review." *Alcoholism: Clinical and Experimental Research* 21 (6): 1073–1082.

Crippa J. A., A. W. Zuardi, R. Martín-Santos, S. Bhattacharyya, Z. Atakan, P. McGuire, and P. Fusar-Poli. 2009. "Cannabis and Anxiety: A Critical Review of the Evidence." *Human Psychopharmacology* 24 (7): 515–523.

Di Domenico, S. I., and R. M. Ryan. 2017. "The Emerging Neuroscience of Intrinsic Motivation: A New Frontier in Self-Determination Research." *Frontiers in Human Neuroscience* 11: 145.

Emanuele, M. A., and N. V. Emanuele. 1998. "Alcohol's Effects on Male Reproduction." *Alcohol Health and Research World* 22 (3): 195–201.

Evans, R. L. 1971. *Richard Evans' Quote Book: Selected from the "Spoken Word" and "Thought for the Day" and from Many Inspiring Thought-Provoking Sources from Many Centuries.* Salt Lake City, UT: Publishers Press.

Fitzgerald, P. J. 2013. "Elevated Norepinephrine May Be a Unifying Etiological Factor in the Abuse of a Broad Range of Substances: Alcohol, Nicotine, Marijuana, Heroin, Cocaine, and Caffeine." *Substance Abuse: Research and Treatment* 7: 171–183.

Gaudiano, B. A. 2008. "Cognitive-Behavioural Therapies: Achievements and Challenges." *Evidence-Based Mental Health* 11 (1): 5–7.

Gjevestad, G. O., K. B. Holven, and S. M. Ulven. 2015. "Effects of Exercise on Gene Expression of Inflammatory Markers in Human Peripheral Blood Cells: A Systematic Review." *Current Cardiovascular Risk Reports* 9 (7): 34.

Gooley, J. J., K. Chamberlain, K. A. Smith, S. B. Khalsa, S. M. Rajaratnam, E. van Reen, J. M. Zeiter, C. A. Czeisler, and S. W. Lockley. 2011. "Exposure to Room Light Before Bedtime Suppresses Melatonin Onset and Shortens Melatonin Duration in Humans." *Journal of Clinical Endocrinology and Metabolism* 96 (3): E463–E472.

Grassian, S. 2006. "Psychiatric Effects of Solitary Confinement." *Washington University Journal of Law and Policy* 22 (1): 325–347.

Hill K., M. Barton, and A. M. Hurtado. 2009. "The Emergence of Human Uniqueness: Characters Underlying Behavioral Modernity." *Evolutionary Anthropology* 18 (5): 187–200.

Jenkins, T. A., J. C. Nguyen, K. E. Polglaze, and P. P. Bertrand. 2016. "Influence of Tryptophan and Serotonin on Mood and Cognition with a Possible Role of the Gut-Brain Axis." *Nutrients* 8 (1): E56.

Karlsson, H. 2011. "How Psychotherapy Changes the Brain." *Psychiatric Times* 28 (8): 8.

Kiser, D., B. Steemers, I. Branchi, and J. R. Homberg. 2012. "The Reciprocal Interaction Between Serotonin and Social Behaviour." *Neuroscience and Biobehavioral Reviews* 36 (2): 786–798.

Koob, G. F. 1996. "Hedonic Valence, Dopamine and Motivation." *Molecular Psychiatry* 1 (3): 186–189.

Leafscience. 2018. "Marijuana and Dopamine: What's the Link?" January 3, 2018. https://www.leafscience.com/2018/01/03/marijuana-dopamine-whats-link.

Lieberman, M. D. 2013. *Social: Why Our Brains Are Wired to Connect.* New York: Crown.

Lieberman, M. D. 2007. "Social Cognitive Neuroscience: A Review of Core Processes." *Annual Review of Psychology* 58: 259–289.

Lindhom, M. E., F. Marabita, D. Gomez-Cabrero, H. Rundqvist, T. J. Ekström, J. Tegnér, and C. J. Sundberg. 2014. "An Integrative Analysis Reveals Coordinated Reprogramming of the Epigenome and the Transcriptome in Human Skeletal Muscle After Training." *Epigenetics* 9 (12): 1557–1569.

Linköping Universitet. 2016. "Brain Volume Changes After Cognitive Behavioral Therapy." *ScienceDaily*. February 2,

2016. www.sciencedaily.com/releases/2016/02/160202185 552.htm.

Ma, H., and G. Zhu. 2014. "The Dopamine System and Alcohol Dependence." *Shanghai Archives of Psychiatry* 26 (2): 61–68.

Nettleton, J. A., I. A. Brouwer, J. M. Geleijnse, and G. Hornstra. 2017. "Saturated Fat Consumption and Risk of Coronary Heart Disease and Ischemic Stroke: A Science Update." *Annals of Nutrition and Metabolism* 70 (1): 26–33.

NH DHHS (New Hampshire Department of Health and Human Services). 2014. "How Much Sugar Do You Eat? You May Be Surprised!" *Health Promotion in Motion.* August 2014. https://www.dhhs.nh.gov/dphs/nhp/documents/sugar.pdf.

NIH (National Institutes of Health). 2013. "How Sleep Clears the Brain." NIH Research Matters. October 28, 2013. https://www.nih.gov/news-events/nih-research-matters/how-sleep-clears-brain.

NIMH (National Institute of Mental Health). 2017. "Major Depression Definitions." Updated November 2017. https://www.nimh.nih.gov/health/statistics/major-depression.shtml.

NIMH (National Institute of Mental Health). 2008. "Sequenced Treatment Alternatives to Relieve Depression (STAR*D) Study." https://www.nimh.nih.gov/funding/clinical-research/practical/stard/index.shtml.

Okamoto-Mizuno, K., and K. Mizuno. 2012. "Effects of Thermal Environment on Sleep and Circadian Rhythm." *Journal of Physiological Anthropology* 31 (1): 14.

Power, M. L., and J. Schulkin. 2009. *The Evolution of Obesity*. Baltimore: Johns Hopkins University Press.

Raposa, E. B., H. B. Laws, and E. B. Ansell. 2016. "Prosocial Behavior Mitigates the Negative Effects of Stress in Everyday Life." *Clinical Psychological Science* 4 (4): 691–698.

Rönn, T., P. Volkov, C. Davegårdh, T. Dayeh, E. Hall, A. H. Olsson et al. 2013. "A Six Months Exercise Intervention Influences the Genome-Wide DNA Methylation Pattern in Human Adipose Tissue." *PLOS Genetics* 9 (6): e1003572.

Sharma, S., and S. Fulton. 2013. "Diet-Induced Obesity Promotes Depressive-Like Behaviour That Is Associated with Neural Adaptations in Brain Reward Circuitry." *International Journal of Obesity* 37 (3): 382–389.

Shepard, R. F. 1979. "'Duke, an American Hero." *New York Times*, June 12. https://archive.nytimes.com/www.nytimes.com/learning/general/onthisday/bday/0526.html?mcubz=3.

Shilo, L., H. Sabbah, R. Hadari, S. Kovatz, U. Weinberg, S. Dolev, Y. Dagan, and L. Shenkman. 2002. "The Effects of Coffee Consumption on Sleep and Melatonin Secretion." *Sleep Medicine* 3 (3): 271–273.

Stein, M. D., and P. D. Friedmann. 2005. "Disturbed Sleep and Its Relationship to Alcohol Use." *Substance Abuse* 26 (1): 1–13.

Thorén, P., J. S. Floras, P. Hoffmann, and D. R. Seals. 1990. "Endorphins and Exercise: Physiological Mechanisms and Clinical Implications." *Medicine and Science in Sports and Exercise* 22 (4): 417–428.

Werner, C., M. Hanhoun, T. Widmann, A. Kazakov, A. Semenov, J. Pöss et al. 2008. "Effects of Physical Exercise on Myocardial Telomere-Regulating Proteins, Survival Pathways, and Apoptosis." *Journal of the American College of Cardiology* 52 (6): 470–482.

World Hunger. 2015. "World Child Hunger Facts." Updated July 2015. https://www.worldhunger.org/world-child-hunger -facts.

Yang, A., Palmer, A., & de Wit, H. (2010). "Genetics of Caffeine Consumption and Responses to Caffeine. *Psychopharmacology* 211 (3): 245–257.

Jonas A. Horwitz, PhD, received a doctorate in clinical psychology from Virginia Commonwealth University, where he conducted extensive research on adults who wrestle with chronic depressive disorders. He is a member of the American Psychological Association, The North Carolina Psychological Association, and the American Academy of Psychotherapists. He maintains a private practice in Durham, NC.

MORE BOOKS *from*
NEW HARBINGER PUBLICATIONS

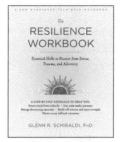